Head of Krishna. Paper cartoon, Jaipur. 2 ft. 18 c. Metropolitan
Museum of Art, Rogers Fund, 1918, New York City.

THE
ARTS & CRAFTS OF INDIA & CEYLON

BY

ANANDA K. COOMARASWAMY

CONTAINING

TWO HUNDRED & TWENTY-FIVE ILLUSTRATIONS

FARRAR, STRAUS AND COMPANY

NEW YORK

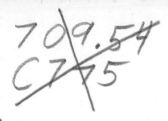
Introduction and Index copyright © 1964, by
Doña Luisa Coomaraswamy

Library of Congress Catalog Number: 64-18969

Manufactured in the United States of America

INTRODUCTION (1963)

"These are our works, these works our souls display;
Behold our works when we have passed away."

THE book is being reprinted after fifty years. Dr.
Ananda K. Coomaraswamy continued to present the
same theses, wording his convictions even more
firmly, with the passing years.

The study of the traditional arts of the Orient and
the Occident to the *philosophia perennis* is the personal history of this man. He bridged the East and
the modern West as few men have wanted to, and
fewer yet have done.

He was born in Ceylon in 1877. His father was a
prominent Hindu and his mother an accomplished
Englishwoman. He was taken to England at the age
of two or three; when his father died in Ceylon, the
mother and child remained in England. He was educated in England and took his doctorate in geology
from the University of London in 1906. By this time
he was already aware of the innate imbalance and
frustration of modern life, and sympathetic to the
currents of the implied references in a traditional
order. He made himself familiar with the landmarks
of traditional and epic literatures of both East and
West.

Observation of the blighting influence of European civilization on the cultures of the East, India
and Ceylon, led him to devote some years to journal-
istic, social and political activities.

The movement from natural sciences to active
participation in the national revivals of India and
especially Ceylon, was dictated in part by his great

concern over social and economic conditions of these countries.

During these early years he produced *Mediaeval Sinhalese Art,** (1908), *The Indian Craftsman, Essays in National Idealism* (1909), *Selected Examples of Indian Art, Indian Drawings* (1910), *Art and Swadeshi* (1911), *Viśvakarma: Examples of Indian Architecture, Sculpture, Painting, Handicrafts* (1912) and the present work (1913). As an art historian Coomaraswamy was (and is) recognized as an unquestionable master.

The true measure of Coomaraswamy's thought can only be gauged in his later work on comparative religions and metaphysics to which he brought his scientific training, competence and intellectual disposition.

Those who are familiar with the early writings only know an aspect and a fragment of this work. It is in the almost incomparable output of his last fifteen years for which the whole of his life effort was a preparation which necessitates and justifies our interest in the earlier work.

The Arts and Crafts of India and Ceylon is a very valuable introduction to Indian art, and to the writings of Coomaraswamy. Those who may be content with this book alone can be confident of the best guide possible. Those who will go further will be fortified, each in his own tradition. The critical reader may be advised that the present work is not yet the mature Coomaraswamy, speaking with most complete awareness of theology, doctrine, symbolism and metaphysics. Some statements expressed in

* Reprinted by Pantheon Books, 1956.

the first chapter were later outgrown, and yet the reader has to know the Coomaraswamy of 1913 to understand the man of 1947.

Coomaraswamy's views on democracy, trade, erotic art, connoisseurship, express his humaneness and his generosity. There are a few comments, minor archaisms, much outdated in 1963, but current over fifty years ago; these have been retained because of their interest.

The extraordinary production in art history, aesthetic theory, social criticism, comparative religion, symbolism and metaphysics of this man is astounding. He had intellectual powers with which few men of his generation could compare. He looked with hope, as we do, for many scholars, in this, our own day, and times to come. His scholarship received the most profound justification, in his own lifetime, rare as this may be.

These various disciplines were to lead him to wholeness of Self; and to lead others to the same fair path—
for "Does the calligrapher write artistically for the sake of writing and not for the sake of the reading?"

DOÑA LUISA COOMARASWAMY

(MRS. ANANDA K. COOMARASWAMY)

December 16, 1963

PREFACE TO THE FIRST EDITION

THE purpose of this book, like that of Professor Flinders Petrie in the same series, is to facilitate the understanding of the art it illustrates. It is intended for ordinary persons rather than for archæological specialists. The pages are not burdened with references; but no statement has been made without careful consideration or specific authority. The value of a small book must depend on its suggestiveness rather than on its completeness: but it must not be forgotten that what is here said is but a mere summary of a vast subject: each sentence could be expanded to a chapter, each chapter to a monograph. If the first chapter should appear long in proportion to those which describe the actual works, which are after all best described in the illustrations, it is because in order to account for Indian, just as for Gothic, "we have to account for its historic basis and for the whole atmosphere of mysticism, chivalry, and work enthusiasm, with all the institutions, romantic and social, which formed its environment" (Professor Lethaby, *Mediæval Art*).

The scope of the book is indicated in its title. Ceylon, from the standpoint of ethnology and culture, is an integral part of India. I have passed beyond the Indian boundary only to include the sculpture of Jāva and Cambodia, the most important of the Ind-

ian colonies: I have not discussed either the architecture or the minor crafts of these countries, nor of
Cambodia, Siam, or Burma, although Burma is now
politically united to India. On the other hand, since
the Himālayas are the natural boundary, the art of
Nepāl, whence come so many fine works often described as Tibetan, is rightly called Indian.

That the work is divided into two parts, the first
concerned with Hindū and Buddhist art, the latter
with the Musulmān arts, is solely to facilitate an understanding of their historical relations and psycho-
logical development: I do not forget that in almost
every art and craft, as also in music, there exists in
Hindustān a complete and friendly fusion of the two
cultures. The non-sectarian character of the styles
of Indian art has indeed always been conspicuous;
so that it is often only by special details that one can
distinguish Jain from Buddhist *stūpas*, Buddhist from
Hindū sculpture, or the Hindū from the Musulmān
minor crafts. The one great distinction of Mughal
from Hindū art is not so much racial as social; the
former is an art of courts and connoisseurs, owing
much to individual patronage, the latter belongs as
much to the folk as to the kings.

It is indeed a most striking feature of Hindū and
Buddhist civilisation that it produced not merely a

great learning somewhat jealously guarded by pandits, but also a religious and æsthetic culture in which all classes shared. "Their ordinary *Plowmen* and *Husbandmen*," says Robert Knox, "do speak elegantly and are full of complement. And there is no difference between the ability and speech of a *Countryman* and a *Courtier*." Such is the natural fruit of feudal and theocratic cultures; a division into classes without tastes or interests in common is characteristic only of a large democracy.

The Hindūs have never believed in art for art's sake; their art, like that of mediæval Europe, was an art for love's sake. They made no distinctions of sacred and profane. I am glad to think that they have never consciously sought for beauty; just as none of their social institutions were intended to promote the greatest happiness of the greatest number. For great art results from the impulse to express certain clear intuitions of life and death, rather than from the conscious wish to make beautiful pictures or songs. The absence of beauty from art, or happiness from life, is an unanswerable condemnation of any civilisation in which they are lacking: yet neither beauty nor happiness is easily attainable if sought for as a primary end. Very often, as in India, they appear like angels unawares, just where the seeming rigidity of hieratic laws would appear to deny all personal freedom. We are forced to think that freedom has other than democratic meanings, and that art has little to do with personal self-expression.

Professor Lethaby has lately written that " If we (in Europe) would set seriously to work in reviving decorative design, the best thing we could do would be to bring a hundred craftsmen from India to form a school of decorative design." But it is well to remember, that if this is still true, it will not be true for long; for nearly every force at work and every tendency apparent in modern India is consciously or unconsciously directed towards the destruction of all skilful handicraft. Neither Nationalist nor Imperialist educators are concerned with that all-important part of education described by Ruskin as the cherishing of local associations, and hereditary skill. I could wish to persuade these teachers that education appears as much in doing as in knowing things —that craftsmanship is a mode of thought, for

> All these trust to their hands:
> And everyone is wise in his work.

ANANDA K. COOMARASWAMY.

CONTENTS

PART ONE
HINDU AND BUDDHIST ART

PART TWO
MUGHAL ART

PART ONE
HINDU & BUDDHIST ART

CHAPTER ONE
INDIAN CHARACTER & HISTORY

1. Natarāja. Abt. 4 ft. 10-12 c. Copper. So. India. Government Museum, Madras.

2. Buddha. Colossal. 3-4 c. Dolomite. Anurādhapura, Ceylon.

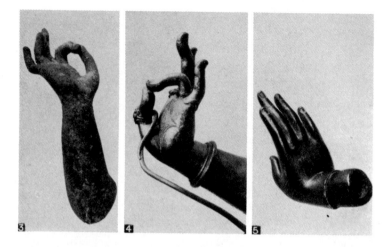

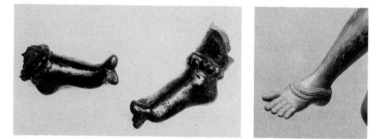

3. Hand of a Buddha. 6 c. Bronze. Buddhavānī. British Museum, London.

4. Hand of a Tārā. 15-18 c. Bronze. Nepāl. Mahārāja of Cossimbazar.

5. Hand of a Buddha. 12-15 c. Copper. Museum of Fine Arts, Boston.

6-7. Feet of Natarāja. 9-10 c. Copper. Anurādhapura. Colombo Museum, Ceylon.

8. Foot of Natarāja. 17-18 c. Copper. Museum of Fine Arts, Boston.

9-12. Gestures: conventional gestures of a dancing girl, Tanjore. 9—"Deer." 10—"Lifting Mount Govardhan." 11—"Garuda [a mythical bird]." 12—"A [four-legged] bed."

13. A damascener. 19-20 c. Jaffna, Ceylon.
14. An architect. 20 c. Tanjore District, So. India.
15. Weavers, 20 c. Madurā, So. India.

16. Seal (impression). Carnelian, king on wicker throne, from
Yatthālā Dāgaba, Ceylon. .78 in. 2 c. B.C. (?). Manchester
Museum, England.

17. Capital of Asoka. Chunār stone. 7 ft. x 2 ft. 10 in. Column.
3 c. B.C. Sandstone. Sārnāth, Sārnāth Museum.

18. Seal (impression). Terra-cotta. Bhītā. 3 in. Archaeological
Survey of India.

ARTS & CRAFTS OF INDIA & CEYLON
BY ANANDA K. COOMARASWAMY
CHAPTER THE FIRST
INDIAN CHARACTER AND HISTORY

THE OLDEST INHABITANTS OF INDIA are known to us by their stone and copper implements and pottery; they survive in the wild hill and forest tribes of many parts of India, and form quantitively the most important factor in the origin of all those who are known now as Indians. Of the mainly non-Āryan Indians, the most important modern representatives are the Dravidians, especially the Tamils and Sinhalese, who already possessed a highly developed civilisation when the first Āryan teachers reached them, some centuries B.C. The origin of these Dravidians is not certainly known. Their language type is as distinct from that of the primitive tribes as it is from that of the Āryans: hence they may perhaps be considered as representatives of prehistoric immigrants rather than strictly aboriginal.

The origin of the Indian Āryans is also greatly disputed. All that it is necessary to know for our present purposes is that in early times the Indo-Āryans who heard the *Vedas* were settled in the Panjāb, the Land of Five Rivers. Their religious poems, the *Vedas*, are the oldest Indian scriptures,

5

consisting of hymns, spells, and ritual ordinances, with traces of advanced philosophical speculation in the later works. The earliest hymns are probably older than 1500 B.C. The essential character of Vedic religion is the worship of the personified powers of nature, *e.g.* Sūrya (Sun), Varuna (Sky), Indra (Rain), Ushas (Dawn), and the more anthropomorphic conception of Yama (Death). A little later there appears a tendency to regard these names as representing the various manifestations of one Spirit, Ātman or Brahmă (neuter), variously personified as Prajāpati (Lord of Creatures), Vishvakarmā (All-fashioner), Purusha (Male), Hiranyagarbha (Golden Womb), and finally as Brahmā (m.).

By the time the Āryans had advanced further, and were permanently settled in the Middle Land of the Upper Ganges valley, there grew out of the *Vedas* the later religion of Brāhmanism, on the one side elaborately ritualistic, on the other profoundly philosophical. The scriptures of this period (800 to 300 B.C.) are the *Brāhmanas* (ritual) and the *Upanishads* (philosophy), forming the last part of the *Vedas*. The *Brāhmanas* are the service-books of the professional and hereditary priests, the Brāhmans. Great stress is laid on the importance of sacrifices and the use of magic formulas, known as *mantras*. These

6

works are of much significance in the history of the
arts: for the exact prescription of altar measurements
may be regarded as the beginning of the *Shilpashāstras*, the ritual demanded the manufacture of
lamps and sacrificial vessels, and the *mantras*, subsequently regarded as independent centres of consciousness, developed into personal divinities with
images and ritual service of their own. The *Upanishads*, with the later interpretations, constitute the
Vedānta (Veda's end), the monistic philosophy which
forms the background to all later Indian mythologies and interpretations of life. Two very important doctrines were generally accepted before the
time of Buddha: *karma* (deeds), that every action
bears inevitable fruit in this life or another, and
samsāra (wandering), that individual souls pass from
body to body in an everlasting wheel of experience.
The *Vedānta* also maintains the illusory character
of the phenomenal world, either as wholly unreal
(*māyā*), or at least as necessarily misapprehended
by finite beings, from whom all absolute truth is
concealed by plural perception or ignorance (*avidyā*).
Salvation is liberation from this wheel of rebirth,
and bondage of ignorance.

Side by side with this idealism grew up the his-
torically only a little less important system of the

Sāmkhya, which postulates an eternal dualism of soul (*Purusha*) and matter (*Prakriti*), without any deity. The founder of this system was Kapila, who if a historical person at all, certainly belongs to the ante-Buddhist period. An important element in Sāmkhyan thought is the theory of the three *gunas*, or conditions of matter, respectively *sattva* (light, clear, intellectual), *rajas* (active, strenuous, emotional), and *tamas* (dark, gloomy, inert).

All the elaborate fabric of modern Hinduism is built up on these materials. Its development as a social and theological system continued throughout the Buddhist period, and up to the 12th century A.D., and in some aspects up to the present days of conflict between orthodoxy and modernism. The principal landmarks in this development are the *Yoga* system of Patanjali (*ca.* 200 B.C.); the epics (*Mahābhārata* and *Rāmāyana*, old sagas handled by Brāhman poets some centuries B.C. with various additions, including the *Bhagavad Gītā*, up to 300–400 A.D.); the *Laws of Manu* (establishing the theoretical basis of the caste system); composition of the *Purānas* (mythologies, etc.); the decline and absorption of Buddhism (complete in most parts of India by the 8th century); the development of the southern theology of Shiva (4th to 10th century A.D.); and the

8

rise of the northern cult of Krishna (2nd to 12th century A.D.). Each of these movements is of supreme importance for the history of art.

There are many phases of later Hindū thought, important for the student of art. The term *shvara* (Overlord) designates a supreme personal God, beyond whom is none but the impersonal and unknowable Brahmă or Ātman. *Ishvara* is worshipped in three aspects, as Brahmā (creator), Vishnu (sustainer), and Shiva (destroyer), sometimes united in one triple image (*Trimūrti*). The worship of Brahmā ceased at an early period; there remain two great Hindū groups or sects, the Vaishnava and the Shaiva. Each of these regard their own deity as *Ishvara*: yet, on the other hand, Vishnu and Shiva are often identified. Each of these has a feminine counterpart, or *Shakti* (Energy); creation and manifestation are effected by the interaction of these male and female principles of the cosmos. Vishnu has Lakshmī: Shiva, Pārvatī. The personality of each of these is manifold, each form having a different name. In particular, there are *sāttvic*, *rājasic*, and *tāmasic* forms, which may even be represented together in a single work of art. Some of these forms are those of non-Āryan deities absorbed into the Brāhman theology.

Other important sects are those of the Shāktas

9

(who worship Shakti, the female cosmic principle), the Sauras (who worship the Sun), the Gānapatyas (who worship Ganesha), and the Sikhs (who combine the ideas of Islām with Hindū thought, and do not worship images).

Vaishnava theology is distinguished by its doctrine of *avatāras*, or incarnations. The ten *avatārs* of Vishnu are the ten forms assumed by him, for the establishment of righteousness when need arises. These incarnations are respectively, the Fish, Tortoise, Boar, Man-lion, Dwarf, Parashu-Rāma, Rāma, Krishna, Buddha, and Kalki (who is yet to come). The legends associated with all of these, but especially those of Rāma and Krishna, are frequently illustrated. Vishnu as *Ishvara* is named Nārāyana, and represented as reclining upon the serpent Sheshanāga, who rests on the cosmic ocean : Brahmā is then born from a lotus that springs from Nārāyana's navel. The aspects of Vishnu are gracious and humanistic.

Shiva, though infinitely gracious in certain aspects, is a more terrible and inaccessible God than Vishnu. He is manifested in various forms, but does not assume a human incarnation. He is conceived best as the Dancer, whose dance is Evolution, Continuance, and Involution : also as the Great Yogī, chief of ascetics, absorbed in contemplation, or wandering through the Himālayan forests with Pārvatī and the bull Nandi. Shiva and Pārvatī have two sons, Ganesha and Kārttikeya, gods of wisdom and war respectively. Shiva is very frequently worshipped in the form of the *lingam*, a symbol partly of phallic origin, partly derived from the Buddhist *stūpa*, and generally associated with the *yoni*, or symbol of Shakti.

Vishnu and Shiva are Dionysic and truly spiritual powers, worshipped by those who seek salvation. Beside these, the Hinduism of the *Purānas* also recognises a group of Olympians, the *devas*, who are worshipped, if at all, for material benefits. These dwell in paradise (*svarga*): the chief of them are Indra (king of the gods), Varuna (Ocean), Agni (Fire), Sūrya (Sun), Chandra (Moon) and Yama (Death). The last presides over Hell. Kāmadeva (Desire), is the god of love. Vishvakarmā is no longer Brahmā, but a god or genius of the arts and crafts. Various sages (*rishis*) are associated with the *devas* as their priests. There are also in heaven other orders of beings, as *apsarās* (dancers), *gandharvas* (musicians), and *kinnaras* (bird-men and horse-men): and creatures who are "vehicles" of the gods, as Vishnu's Garuda, Pārvatī's Tiger, Ganesha's Rat, and Indra's Elephant.

11

Vishnu and Shiva are worshipped by the Olympians, as by men, and also by devils. Set over against the *devas* are the devils, variously called *daityas*, *asuras*, or *rākshasas*, with whom the gods are frequently at war. *Nāgas*, or half-human serpents, dwell in the waters and underworlds.

None of these beings are eternal, but all, with men, animals, and the whole animate and "inanimate" creation, are part of the *samsāra*, the ocean of life subject to change. It is in Vishnu or Shiva that all these move and have their being. The demerit and merit of human beings are rewarded successively in Heaven and Hell in the intervals between births on earth. The great contrast between this exoteric system and the ultimate ideal of Hindū thought is well expressed in the saying, that "he who seeks emancipation should fear Heaven no less than Hell." But all forms of Indian thought unite in regarding *ahamkāra*, the sense of egoity or separateness from other living things, as the greatest of all delusions and the source of infinite sufferings.

So far we have postponed the consideration of Buddhism, on the ground that the Buddhist heresy, however important, did not even temporarily interfere with the development of distinctively Hindū modes of thought. The probable dates of Buddha's life are 563 to 483 B.C., the date of his death forming the first quite definite landmark in Indian history. Prince Siddhārtha, afterwards Buddha ("the Enlightened") grew up in the Brāhmanical tradition: he was impressed in early manhood with the problem of suffering: and leaving his royal estate, and independently of the priests, he sought a way of escape from the *samsāra*. As regards doctrine, he took for granted such theories as those of *karma*, and rebirth: he did not deny, but ignored the Olympians of the Brāhmans: he refused to discuss the origins of life, or to speak of things after death: he denied the theory of the *Ātman*, and laid great stress on the conception of life as perpetual change: he denied equally the efficacy of sacrifices, exaggerated asceticism, or prayer, maintaining that the true Path was that of personal morality and intellectual progress. He established an order of begging monks, who have maintained an honourable tradition to the present day in Ceylon and Burma: if he repudiated all unreasonable mortifications, none the less he sought to withdraw from the world as many as possible of the wisest and best of men, to lead a life of very considerable restraint. He could not help but look upon women and all the arts (as music and dancing, etc.) as snares from which men should en-

deavour to escape. He made the sole end of life, salvation (*nirvāna*): a view contrasting with the Hindū
conception of the four ends of life, viz. the practice of
morality (*dharma*), the acquiring of wealth (*artha*),
the satisfaction of desires (*kāma*), and progress towards emancipation (*moksha*). There is therefore
some justification for speaking of Buddha's system as puritanical. His influence on all later Hindū
thought is due largely to the power of his own mag-
netic and gracious personality, and to the essential
value and moderation, rather than to the originality,
of his teaching. But Buddhism became, and must
have become, something more than the philosophy
of Buddha, before it could inspire a great religious
art such as that of Ajantā or Borōbodur.

Early Buddhism (*Hīnayāna*, the "Lesser Vehicle") was soon modified by the mythologising tendency of Indian thought, from the 2nd century B.C.
onwards evolving an elaborate theology (*Mahāyāna*,
the "Great Vehicle"), closely corresponding to that
of the Hindūs. The chief god-types are the Sav-
iours or Future Buddhas (*Bodhisattvas*) and their
Shaktis or female Energies. There are likewise imagined *Dhyāni* (rapt) Buddhas, of whom the earthly
Buddhas are but a mirage or projection—a doctrine
similar to that of the *avatārs*. Ultimately these ex-

hibit placid, stern, and fierce forms like those of the Hindū deities. By the 8th century A.D. Mahāyāna Buddhism had partly fused with and partly been replaced by Hindū theologies in most parts of India: but it survived in Bengal and Orissa until the 13th century or later, and in its most mystic, *Tāntric* form, up to the present day in Nepāl, and in orthodox forms, in Ceylon.

Early Buddhism was carried to Ceylon in the time of Asoka (2nd century B.C.) and has remained to this day the religion of the Sinhalese. During the first six centuries A.D. it was taken, in the Brāhmanised Mahāyāna form, to China, where a great Buddhist art developed on Indian lines; in the 8th century it went with Indian colonists to Jāva, where are to be seen some of the finest works of Buddhist art in existence. Somewhat later, Buddhist and Hindū art and thought were equally firmly established in Burma, Siam, and Cambodia.

The Musulmān raids began at the close of the 10th century : the Mughal power was only firmly established in the time of Bābur (16th century). Islām contrasts with Hindūism, as a clear-cut monotheism, strongly opposed to all kinds of image worship, and even to the representation of living objects in works of art. In one aspect, Islām is fanatical and puritanical, and thus destructive of Hindū culture where-ever possible: in another (Sūfīism), it closely approaches, and even fuses with, Hindū thought.

The Parsīs, a small community of Zoroastrians settled in the west of India, have had no direct influence on the history of Indian art. But the Zoroastrian and Āryan mythologies go back to common origins.

Let us now discover the working out of the ideas of which the development has been already outlined. In the first place, almost all Hindū art (Brāhmanical and Mahāyāna Buddhist) is religious. "Even a mis-shapen image of a god," says Sukrāchārya (*ca.* 5th century A.D.) "is to be preferred to an image of a man, howsoever charming." Not only are images of men condemned, but originality, divergence from type, the expression of personal sentiment, are equally forbidden. "(An image made) according to rule (*shāstra*) is beautiful, no other forsooth is beautiful: some (deem) that beautiful which follows after (their own) fancy, but that not according to the rule (appears) unlovely to the discerning." The spirit of these uncompromising doctrines lies at the root of the Hindū view of art: these limitations and this discipline are the source of its power. Let us study its expression in a few concrete examples.

CHARACTER AND HISTORY

The Hindūs do not regard the religious, æsthetic, and scientific standpoints as necessarily conflicting, and in all their finest work, whether musical, literary, or plastic, these points of view, nowadays so sharply distinguished, are inseparably united.

This synthesis is nowhere better realised than in the image of Natarāja (fig. 1), "Lord of the Dance," a form of Shiva, as Overlord, *Īshvara*. From references to Natarāja in the contemporary hymns we learn the precise significance of the images, and gather that this significance must have been quite familiar to the imagers themselves and to the worshippers. In these images, Shiva has four arms; his braided locks whirl in the dance. Set in the hair are a cobra, a skull, a mermaid figure of the Ganges, and the crescent moon; in the right ear is a man's earring, in the left a woman's; one hand holds a drum, and another fire, while one is raised, and the fourth points to the lifted foot. The right foot is pressed upon a dwarf: from the lotus pedestal rises an encircling glory, fringed with flame, and touched by the hands holding drum and fire. The images are of all sizes, from a few inches to four feet in height: the splendid example illustrated is one of the largest. The interpretation of the dance is as follows: In the Night of Brahmā, Nature is inert, and cannot dance till Shiva wills it: He rises from his stillness, and, dancing, sends through matter pulsing waves of awakening sound, proceeding from the drum: then Nature also dances, appearing about him as a glory (this glory, the *tiruvāsi*, is broken away from the example illustrated). Then in the fulness of time, still dancing, He destroys all Names and Forms by Fire, and there is new rest. Thus Time and the Timeless are reconciled by the conception of phase alternations extending over vast areas of space and great tracts of time. The orderly dance of the spheres, the perpetual movement of atoms, evolution and involution, are conceptions that have at all times recurred to men's minds; but to represent them in the visible form of Natarāja's Dance is a unique and magnificent achievement of the Indians.

If the dancing figure stands for evolution, the everlasting becoming, the *yogī* type of the seated Buddha (fig. 2) is an equally dramatic image of withdrawal, of complete independence, of involution. It is well to remember that this pose does not represent any sort of mortification of the flesh: it is simply that position which has been immemorially adopted by Indian thinkers, as most convenient for meditation, because the body remains self-supported without effort, and on the other hand without a tendency to sleep.

18

How little this stillness is related to inertia appears in the familiar simile : "the likeness of the seated *yogī* is a lamp in a windless place that flickers not" (*Bhagavad Gītā*, vi. 19). It is just this likeness that we must look for in the Buddha image, and this only. For the Buddha statue was not intended to represent a man; it was to be like the unwavering flame, an image of what all men could become, not the similitude of any apparition (*nirmānakāya*).

A like impersonality appears in the facial expression of all the finest Indian sculptures. These have sometimes been described as expressionless because they do not reflect the individual peculiarities which make up expression as we commonly conceive it. When, however, we "look to those qualities which in their literature were held up as the ideals of life" (Flinders Petrie, *The Arts and Crafts of Ancient Egypt*), we begin to understand the facial expression of Hindū images. This ideal is described in many places, typically, for example, in the *Bhagavad Gītā* xi. 12–19 : "Hateless toward all born beings, void of the thought of I and My, bearing indifferently pain and pleasure, before whom the world is not dismayed and who is not dismayed before the world; who rejoices not, grieves not, desires not; indifferent in honour and dishonour, heat and cold, joy and pain; free from attachment "—such an one is god-like, " dear to Me," says Krishna. The *Bhagavad Gītā* is also the chief gospel of action without attachment: change, says Krishna, is the law of life, therefore act according to duty, not clinging to any object of desire, but like the actor in a play, who knows that his mask (*persona*-lity) is not himself.

For this impassivity is not less characteristic of the faces of the gods in moments of ecstatic passion or destroying fury, than of the face of the stillest Buddha. In each, emotion is interior, and the features show no trace of it: only the movements or the stillness of the limbs express the immediate purpose of the actor. That it is "this body," not the inmost Self that acts, "that slayeth or is slain," is as clearly expressed in the Indian sculpture of the golden age, as anywhere in Vedic literature. This amazing serenity (*shānti*) in moments of deepest passion is not quite confined to Indian sculpture: something very like it, and more familiar to Western students, is found in the gracious and untroubled Mænad furies of the Greek vases, the irresponsible and sinless madness of the angry Bacchæ—

"Is it joy or terror, ye storm-swift feet?"

But how far away is this Indian and early Greek calm from the violence of the Laocoon and from the mod-

ern concept of the "man of action"! It is a far journey
from the art of personality and self-expression, to the
art that reveals a Self not involved in any of its transient empirical activities, howsoever noble or base in
outward seeming.

I do not mean to say that all these deep thoughts
were consciously expressed by every craftsman; certainly not when tradition had become a mere habit.
But, to adapt slightly the words of Nietzsche, those
who first uttered these thoughts in stone or metal,
and some of those who came after them, knew as well
as the wisest ones about the secret of life. The view
of life that irradiated the whole mental atmosphere
of India could not be absent from her art; if we realise this, we must become aware that to seek for a
likeness to men, or the expression of transient sentiment, in Indian art, is merely to seek for its weak
moments.

Images such as the dancing Shiva or the seated
Buddha are the work of a school, not of any one artist.
All essential details are passed on from father to son
in pupillary succession through successive generations, the medium of transmission consisting of example, exact formulas in Sanskrit verse, and diagram-
matic sketches. Thus during many centuries the
artists of one district apply themselves to the inter-

pretation of the same ideas; the origin of those ideas
is more remote than any particular example. The
great types are the fruit of communal rather than individual thought. This communal thought, however,
is not only popular thought, but that of the greatest
and wisest minds of successive generations seeking
to impress their vision on a whole race.

There is no more remarkable illustration of the
Hindū perception of the relative insignificance of the
individual personality, than the fact that we scarcely
know the name of a single painter or sculptor of the
great periods: while it was a regular custom of authors to ascribe their work to better-known authors, in
order to give a greater authority to the ideas they
set forth. The absence of names in the history of
Indian art is a great advantage to the historian of
art; for he is forced to concentrate all his attention
upon their work, and its relation to life and thought
as a whole, while all temptation to anecdotal criticism is removed.

When such types become stereotyped, or the individual craftsman is a poor artist, the æsthetic value
of any particular image is proportionately lessened.
But experience proves that for most of the innocent,
religious significance is scarcely reduced by the æsthetic decadence of a declining style or the crude

ferior craftsmen, who in any case would produce inferior versions of the great motifs, if thrown wholly upon their own resources, would also come short in science and in devotion, and produce works not merely æsthetically worthless, but altogether worthless. This is, in fact, the diagnosis of the shortcoming of all our modern individualistic art, that seven-eighths of it is the work of men who ought to be servants, and not masters : while the work of the one-eighth (if there be so large a proportion of genius) is necessarily intelligible only to a very small audience.

Yet there is one fatal weakness of the later phases of a traditional art : it has no power to resist the corruption from without. It is beautiful by habit rather than intention, so that a single generation under changed conditions is sufficient to destroy it. The caste system and the hieratic sanctions of Indian design have protected Indian handicraft for a time : but it would be useless to pretend that these handicrafts, for all their splendour and devotion, any longer represent the thought and feeling of new India. Ninety-nine of a hundred university-educated Indians are perfectly indifferent to them. The overwhelming desire of modern India is to be like modern Europe : it will be many weary centuries before her people are once again of one mind, or have so clear a vision of life

it possible to find any true short way to art, it would
surely be this, that the artist must identify himself
with his subject; it should be an insult to credit him
with observation, for to observe implies a separation
from that which is observed. It is likewise a test of
art, that it should enable the spectator to forget himself, and to become its subject, as he does in dreams.
But this method is not really a short one. "Only when
I was seventy-three," says Hokusai, "had I got some
sort of insight into the real structure of nature . . .
at the age of eighty I shall have advanced still further;
at ninety, I shall grasp the mystery of things ; at a
hundred, I shall be a marvel, and at a hundred and ten
every blot, every line from my brush shall be alive."

It is not, of course, to be supposed that every minor
craftsman always followed out the ritual prescribed
for the artist, or that the ritual never degenerated
into a mere formula: but the theory no doubt actually represents the mental attitude of those who first
saw the great motifs, as truly as it represents the
position of those who heard the Vedas. All these,
sculptors, poets, or singers, desired to make themselves a channel for the passage of ideas from a divine
world to this physical earth, and all equally regarded
personal and discrete intellectual activity as incompatible with the apprehension of remote truth.

of the hands). Such symbols belong to the category of things taken for granted by the artist, and it is only because we conceive them pedantically that we fail to realise how easy it was to endow them with life.

Countless human and racial associations gather about the lotus: its delicate blossoms are the glory of every bathing pool and lake, while in literature the eyes of every beautiful woman or man are likened to its flowers, and these flowers, closing at night and imprisoning the bees, are the constant subject of other poetic metaphors. Growing in the mud, and yet so clean, the lotus is a symbol of purity: a lotus-pool, with leaves and flowers in bud, widely opened, and again dying down, is an image of the ebb and flow of human life (*samsāra*). Bodily centres of consciousness, such as the solar plexus, the heart and the brain, are represented in lotus forms, while the whole universe is sometimes imagined as one great flower whose petals are outlined by the starry worlds: in this last sense, probably, we should understand the flower held in the hand of Avalokiteshvara and other deities, the flowers offered by the *gopīs* to Krishna, and those offered in daily worship. Most important, however, in art, is the representation of a lotus flower as the seat of a god, or beneath the feet of a standing figure of a god, a convention representing the

to one who has never seen them in life. To take concrete examples, the right hand of fig. 28 is in *vitarka
mudrā*, indicating argument or discourse ; the nearer right hand of fig. 1, the right hand of fig. 35, and
the detached hand of fig. 5, are in *abhaya mudrā*, indicating "do not fear"; the hands of fig. 24 are in the
dharma-cakra mudrā, "turning the wheel of the
Law"; the pose of fig. 31 is known as *mahārāja-līlā-
āsana*, " pose of kingly ease." The three most usual
variations of the seated Buddha or yogī type are (1)
with the hands folded in the lap, in *dhyāni mudrā*,
"meditation"(fig. 2); (2) the right hand raised in discourse (figs. 3, 4); and the right hand dropped over
the knee to touch the earth (*bhūmishparsa mudrā*,
"calling earth to witness"). A less formal treatment
of the hands in other works is often no less eloquent;
for example, the hand of Pārvāti laid on Shiva's arm
(fig. 30); the offering hands of Hanuman (fig. 49);
the praying hands of the *nāginīs* (fig. 70); the sing-
er's fingers (fig. 71); and the dancing feet of Shiva
(figs. 6–8). Such hands and limbs of Indian images
reflect the Indian physical type in their smoothness
and flexibility, and the nervousness of their vitality.
There, every separate finger, whether motionless or
moving, is alive; while it is one of the clearest signs
of decadence and reduced intensity of realisation,

when the fingers become either stiff or flabby, or disposed exactly in one plane.

Beside the seated forms already noticed, there are not less characteristic standing poses. Some severe types are perfectly symmetrical (figs. 27, 51); but more frequent, and capable of greater variation, is the stance, well seen in fig. 57, where the weight of the body rests on one leg and the other is slightly bent. Images of the latter type are called *trivanka*, because the median line, in front view, is thrice curved. A variety of this with legs crossed is frequently adopted in the representations of Krishna as flute-player (figs. 58, 132). From such forms, again, there are all transitions to the continuous movement and perfect fluidity of the dancers (fig. 1, etc.). If any power in Indian art is really unique, it is its marvellous representation of movement—for here in the movement of the limbs is given the swiftness and necessity of the impelling thought itself, much more than a history of action subsequent to thought.

There is a close connection between sculpture and dancing; not merely inasmuch as certain images represent dancing gods (Shiva, Krishna, etc.), but because the Indian art of dancing is primarily one of gesture, in which the hands play a most important part. The special symbolism of hands (*mudrā*) has

31

been already alluded to (p. 29); but only a complete knowledge of the language of dance gesture would prepare the student to fully interpret the sculptures (*cf.* figs. 1, 50). Four positions of the hands photographed from a bayadère of Tanjore are given here as examples, the figs. 9–12 signifying respectively a deer, Krishna's raising Mount Govardhan, Vishnu's Garuda, and a bed. By means of this concrete gesture language the dancer is enabled to give long descriptions of the gods, especially the incarnations of Vishnu, and to express every possible sentiment (*rasa*).

A few words may be added here about the status of the craftsman. In Vedic times, the *rishis* themselves are represented as preparing the sacrificial posts and altars; in Asoka's day, those who injured the royal craftsmen were liable to the punishment of death; while it has been a constant feature of Indian civilisation, as of all aristocratic and theocratic cultures, that the craftsmen should be endowed, receiving either royal or ecclesiastical patronage. Craftsmanship, like learning, being thus protected, and the craftsman holding an assured and hereditary position, can alone make possible the association with work of that leisure and affection which distinguish all the finest handicraft.

CHARACTER AND HISTORY

The practice of the arts has usually been confined to the members of hereditary castes. The higher Hindū and Sinhalese artificers trace their descent from Vishvakarmā : to this day they style themselves Vishvabrāhmans, employ priests of their own caste, and claim spiritual equality with Brāhmans. All craftsmen regard their art as a mystery, and look upon its traditions, handed down in pupillary succession, as invested with sacred and scriptural authority. In connection with the consecration of images, the higher craftsmen themselves exercise sacerdotal functions.

The importance attached to craftsmanship, and the picture of the ideal craftsman, may be gathered from the following characteristic extracts from a *Shilpashāstra* :

"That any other than a *Shilpan* should build temples, towns, seaports, tanks, or wells, is comparable to the sin of murder.

" The *Shilpan* should understand the *Atharva Veda*, the 32 *Shilpashāstras*, and the Vedic *mantras* by which the deities are invoked.

" The *Shilpan* should be one who wears a sacred thread, a necklace of sacred beads, and a ring of *kusha* grass upon his finger : one delighting in the worship of God, faithful to his wife, avoiding strange women,

33

true to his family, of a pure heart and virtuous, chanting the *Vedas*, constant in the performance of ceremonial duties, piously acquiring a knowledge of various sciences—such a one is indeed a Craftsman."

We are also told that expert and honest craftsmen and architects will be reborn in royal or noble families: but those who work amiss will fall into hell, and shall return to future lives of poverty and hardship.

It is noteworthy that in many crafts the final product is a result of the division of labour. The craftsman is not often his own designer. The cotton printers and embroiderers do not make their own wood blocks: the painter draws on the cloth or metal the necessary outlines for the Chambā embroiderer or the Ceylon damascener. Brocade patterns are not designed by the actual weavers. The Jaipur enamels are the work of at least five persons—designer, goldsmith, engraver, maker of the enamel, and enameller. Where there is no recourse to an "artist," it will be found that most of the designs are traditionally inherited, and so constant as to be familiar to every workman, and there is little to distinguish the work of one man from another. But the designer is always familiar with the conditions of the craft; there is no division of labour akin to the industrial distinction and separation of the artist from the craftsman. In many cases also it happens that the best men are at once designers and themselves skilled in many crafts: in Ceylon, for example, the same man may be at once an architect, jeweller, painter, and ivory carver.

Already in the time of Buddha the craftsmen were organised in guilds (*sreni*), the number of which is often given as eighteen. In northern India at the present day there are also guilds of Musulmān craftsmen, such as that of the Benares brocade weavers; but the tendency since Mughal times has been for the Hindū workmen to predominate.

We must now return from the actual craftsman to a very brief discussion of political history, in so far as it can form the basis of a classification of schools of art. After Buddha (*d.* 483 B.C.) the next great landmarks of Indian history are Alexander's raid (327 B.C.), the reign of Chandragupta Maurya at Pātaliputra (321–297 B.C.), and the reign of his grandson Asoka, " Beloved of the Gods" (272–235 B.C.). In Asoka's time Buddhism was still essentially a system of rationalistic morality, though already with traces of metaphysical and theological development. To this system Asoka became a convert, and first made of Buddhism a state religion. He also sent missionaries throughout India and to Ceylon, and even to Europe and Africa. Within his own dominions (all India

35

except the extreme south) he set up a number of stone pillars inscribed with edicts enjoining the practice of the Buddhist morality, but without antagonism to other beliefs.

After Asoka, princes of Greek descent occupied Afghanistān and the country west of the Indus. Asiatic tribes known as Sakas and Kushāns then replaced these and invaded and occupied the north-west of India, remaining in power during the first three centuries after Christ. Kanishka's capital (*ca.* 78 A.D.) was at Peshāwar. These " Indo-Scythians " were thoroughgoing Buddhists and patronised a prolific sculpture and architecture based on Roman and late Greek models. The mystic and theological development of Mahāyāna Buddhism was now almost complete.

The next great dynasty was that of the Guptas (320–480 A.D.), whose capital was again at Pātaliputra. Their empire extended across northern India from Kāthiāwār to Bengal. During this period and succeeding centuries, many " White Hūns " from Central Asia invaded India and settled in Rājputāna and the Panjāb, where they were completely Hinduised, and become Rājputs.

Our intimate knowledge of the Guptas is largely due to the Chinese Buddhist pilgrim Fa-Hien (tra-

velled 399–413 A.D.), who lived for six years at Pātaliputra. The Guptas were themselves Vaishnava
Hindūs, but favoured the Buddhists, and Fa-Hien
describes the two cults as flourishing side by side.

The Guptas were followed by Harshavardhana
(606–648 A.D.), and his contemporary Pulakesin in
the Deccan. In his reign Hiouen Tsang (travelled
629–645 A.D.), another Chinese Buddhist pilgrim,
journeyed all over India, and wrote an invaluable account of what he saw. Harshavardhana patronised
all sects, particularly the Shaivites, Sauras, and Buddhists.

The 5th, 6th, and 7th centuries (Guptas and Harsha) cover the most brilliant period of classic Sanskrit
literature and Hindū learning generally; this was
the flowering time of the Hindū renaissance. The
epics had already been completed. Drama reached
its zenith in Kālidāsa (5th century), and for theory,
in Bharata; while this was no doubt also the golden
age of Indian music. Bāna in the 7th century describes a court life exactly like that represented in
the contemporary paintings of Ajantā. The *Shilpashāstras* and other encyclopædic works may also be
assigned to the Gupta period, rather earlier than later.
This was also the chief scientific period of Hindūism,
covering the lives of the three greatest of Indian as-

tronomers. Buddhism meanwhile gradually declined, except locally in Bengal, Nepāl, and Ceylon, absorbed rather than ousted by Hindūism. This was also an age of maritime activity, shown, for example, in the colonisation of Jāva. The Gupta and Harsha period was also one of profound Indian influence upon China, and, somewhat later, Japan. At this time India was the dynamic centre of all Asia and the first civilised power in the whole world.

After Harsha, Northern India was divided into various Rājput kingdoms; this Rājput period lasted till the 12th century, and in areas not overwhelmed by the Muhammadans, viz. in Rājputāna and the Panjāb Himālayas, it continues to the present day. Other Hindū dynasties (Chalukyas, Hoysalas, etc.) occupied the Deccan; while Buddhist kingdoms were maintained in Bengal and Orissa till the 12th century. In the far south (Drāvida) three ancient kingdoms, the Chola, Chera, and Pāndava, maintained an old and independent civilisation distinguished in literary achievement and seaborne trade with Europe and the far East. Southern India is without doubt the Biblical " Ophir."

The chief landmarks of the history of Ceylon are the conversion to Buddhism by Asoka's missionaries (B.C. 307): the capital at Anurādhapura up to the

8th century: at Polonnāruva from the 8th to the 13th century: at Kandy from the 16th century: and the British occupation in 1815. It should be noted that the distinctively Sinhalese (Buddhist) art is the Kandyan art of the interior: the art of Jaffna belongs to that of Southern India, while that of the low country during the last three centuries has been one-third European.

The Musulmān occupation of India falls into two periods, first, the destructive phase, 1000 to 1506 A.D., and second, the Mughal Empire, 1506 to 1761 A.D. The Muhammadans at one time or another over-ran nearly all India except Travancore and Nepāl. The southern Hindū kingdom of Vijanayagar successfully held its own from its rise in the 14th century till its fall in 1565: while the Marattas successfully established their independence in the 18th century, when Mughal power was rapidly declining. The British period is generally held to begin with the year 1761.

Lack of space prohibits any detailed discussion of the foreign elements in Indian art. The most ancient part of this art belongs to the common endowment of "Early Asiatic" culture which once extended from the Mediterranean to China, and as far south as Ceylon, where some of the most archaic motifs sur-

39

vive in the decoration of pottery. To this Mykenean facies belong all the simpler arts of woodwork, weaving, metal-work, pottery, etc., together with a group of designs including many of a remarkably Mediterranean aspect, others more likely originating in Western Asia. The wide extension and consistency of this culture throughout Asia in the second millennium B.C. throws important light on ancient trade intercourse, at a time when the Eastern Mediterranean formed the Western boundary of the civilised world.

Much later in origin are the definite Assyrianisms and Persian elements in the Asokan and early Buddhist sculpture, such as the bell-capital and winged lions. Alexander's raid in 327 B.C. left no permanent effects of any sort on Indian culture; but Greek influences are strong in the first three or four centuries A.D., in the north (Panjāb, Mathurā, and Nepāl). The 6th and 7th centuries are the creative and most independent age of classic Indian art, which culminates in the 8th.

Saracenic influences increase from the time of Mahmūd Ghaznī's first raid in 1000 A.D. up to the 17th century (extending even to Jāva, conquered in 1488 A.D.), while Hindū and Buddhist art in Nepāl, Orissa, Southern India, and Ceylon, were almost unaffected. European influences, chiefly on painting, are clearly distinguishable from the close of the 16th century; in the south and west there is a definite Indo-Portuguese style of wood and metal work. The full destructive force of Western industrialism has not been felt till after 1850: the modern Swadeshi movement, for the revival of Indian manufactures, is but little concerned with handicraft or happiness.

The schools of styles of Indian art as known by actual remains may be classified as follows :

EARLY BUDDHIST, B.C. 300 to 50 A.D.: pillar edicts, Sānchī and Mahābodhi stūpas and railings (all Asokan, 3rd century B.C.); Mathurā fragments; Amarāvatī and Bharhut stūpa, and Sānchī gates (2nd and 1st century B.C.).

KUSHĀN OR GRÆCO-BUDDHIST, 50 to 320 A.D.: Gandhāra sculptures of the Afghanistān frontier; sculpture at Mathurā; architecture at Gandhāra, and later in Kāshmīr (Mārtand, 8th century): Mahābodhi great temple (*ca.* 140 A.D.): Besnagar *garuda* pillar; transition of Early Buddhist to Gupta at Amarāvatī (railing, 150 to 200 A.D.); early painting at Ajantā and in Orissa.

GUPTA, 320 to 600 A.D.: sculpture and architecture (stūpa, etc.), at Sārnāth; at Anurādha-

pura (2nd century B.C. to 9th century A.D.);
sculpture and painting at Ajantā; painting
and secular architecture at Sīgiriya (Ceylon,
5th century).

CLASSIC INDIAN, 600 to 850 A.D., but especially
the 8th century: latest and best painting at
Ajantā; sculpture and architecture at Elūra, Elephanta, Māmallapuram, Anurādhapura and Borōbodur (Jāva).

MEDIÆVAL, 9th to 18th century (surviving in Ceylon, Travancore, Rājputāna, etc., up to the
British period, and in Nepāl to the present day): Shaivite bronzes (Natarāja, etc.);
sculpture and architecture of Tanjore (10th
to 12th century), Vijayanagar (14th to 16th
century), Madura (17th century), Auvadaiyār
Kovil, Tārpatri (16th century), Perūr, Srīran-
gam, Rāmesvaram, etc.; Chalukyan architecture of Mysore, etc. (Belūr, Halebīd, 12th
to 13th century); sculpture and architecture
in Jāva up to 14th century, in Cambodia to
the 12th; Polonnāruva sculpture and architecture (8th to 13th century), Kandy (16th
to 18th century); Jain temples at Ābū (11th
to 13th century), Orissa (Bhuvaneshvar,
Konārak, Purī, 9th to 13th century), Khaj-

urāho (*ca.* 1000 A.D.); Rājput painting and architecture (up to 19th century); Mughal painting and architecture (16th to 18th century); Nepalese Buddhist bronzes; art of Burma and Siam.

BRITISH, 1760–   : decline of crafts; survival of architecture; school-of-art painting; *swadeshi*; modern Bengālī painting.

Hamsa : Tanjore drawing,
20th century.

CHAPTER TWO
SCULPTURE

19. Kuvera (*Yaksha*). 2 c. B.C
Sandstone. Bharhut, India
Museum, Calcutta.

19a. Dryad: *yakshī* or *vrikshakā*. East Gate at Sāñchī, detail showing woman and tree bracket.

20. Buddha teaching. Gandhāra. Schist. 1-2 c. 36 in. British Museum.
21. Bodhisattva. Gandhāra. 2-3 c. 35½ in. Royal Ontario Museum, Toronto.
22. Elevation of the Bowl Relic, "Grail." Amarāvatī. Marble. 3 c. 2 ft. 9¼ in. Government Museum. Madras.
23. Casing slab. Relic Shrine. Marble. Amarāvatī (*stūpa*), Buddhist relic mound. Late 2 c. 6 ft. 2¾ in. Government Museum, Madras.

24. Buddha preaching the First Sermon. White sandstone. 5 ft.
2 in. 5 c. Archaeological Museum, Sārnāth.
25. *Nāga* door-guardian. (Semi-human, semi-serpent.) 6-7 c.
Granulite. Anurādhapura, Ceylon.
26. Stone relief: love-scene or donors. Built into wall at Isurumuniya Vihāra, Anurādhapura, Ceylon.
27. Buddha standing. Crystaline limestone, over life size. 3-4 c.
Ruanveli Dāgaba, Anurādhapura, Ceylon.

28. Avalokiteshvara Bodhisattva. Dhyāni Buddha Amitābha in headdress. Bronze. 8 c. 3½ in. Museum of Fine Arts, Boston.

29. Jambhala Kuvera. Citron in one hand, mongoose in other ejecting coins into container. Bronze. 8 c. 3⅛ in. Museum of Fine Arts, Boston.

30. Shiva and Pārvatī, Mt. Kailāsa temple relief (Upper half). Colossal. Basalt. Elūra. 8 c. Kailāsanātha temple, Kāñcīpuram.

31. The Sage Kapila. Rock-cut seated figure; on the proper right, head of a horse. Granulite, over life size. 8 c. Isurumuniya Vihāra, Anurādhapura, Ceylon.

32. Vishnu-Anantashayin Relief. (Vishnu reclining on the Serpent Ananta [Infinity]). Mahisha (*mandapam*), shrine. Rock-cut, colossal. 7 c. Māmallapuram, near Madras.

33. Maheshvara-mūrti. Three-headed form of the Supreme Shiva: *creation, protection, destruction.* Right and central faces are peaceful (*shānti*), left fierce (*ugra*) aspect. Note skull in headdress, and just below it, cobra-hood. Trap-rock. Colossal, 8 c. Elephanta.

34a. Devī Durgā Mahisha-mardinī (Devī Durgā slaying the demon Mahishāsura). Bronze. 6 in. 9-10 c. Jāva. Leiden Museum.

34. A Sage reading a palm-leaf MS. (Thought to be Parākrama
Bāhu I, or Kapila.) 11-12 c. Rock-cut. 11 ft. 6 in. Polonnāruva,
Ceylon.

35. Dhyāni-Buddha. Stone. 8-10 c. Borōbodur, Jāva.
36. Ganesha (God of wisdom, arts, sciences, "Remover of ob-
    stacles"). Stone. 8-10 c. From Singasari (Jāva). In Wat Paa
    Keo, Bangkok, Siam.
37. Dancer. (Relief, lower part of main wall first gallery on ter-
    race.) 8-10 c. Detail measures 23½ x 18 in. Borōbodur.
38. Buddha or Bodhisattva. Stone. 8-10 c. Cambodia. Trocadero,
    Paris.

39. Woman. 10-12 c. Gwaliar.
40. Tārā (Ushnīsha-Vijaya), 'Saviouress,' 'lotus-born,' like to the
    Blessed Virgin Mary, the 'Mother of God.' Shale. 12 c. Pāla.
    19 in. Sārnāth Museum.
41. Seated figure (Torso and base). Kshatriya type. Sandstone.
    11-12 c. Pāla. Indian Museum, Calcutta.
42. Seated figure (Torso and base). Brahman type. Sandstone.
    11-12 c. Pāla. Indian Museum, Calcutta.

43. Woman. Bhuvaneshvar. 13 c. Formerly collection of Mr. Ponten-Möller, Calcutta.
44. Women (*apsarās*), nymphs or dancing figures. Konārak. 13 c. (projecting pilasters of temple façade).
45. *Pattinī* and *nāga* king. 11-14 c. Wood. Nikawewa, Ceylon.
46. Led horse, Konārak. Sandstone, colossal. 13 c. Led by warrior, the horse tramples a demon (*asura*).

48. Sundara-mūrti Svāmi, Shaiva boy-saint. Copper. 25 in. 12-
13 c. Polonnāruva. Colombo Museum.

50. Bhikshātana Shiva. (Shiva as mendicant.) Copper. Abt. 1800.
40 in. So. India. Museum of Fine Arts, Boston.

51. Figures of Krishna Deva Rāja of Vijayanagar, and his two
queens. Copper. 16 c. (1509-1529 A.D.) Śrīnivāsa Perumāl
temple, Tirumala, Tirupati.

47. Mānikka Vāçagar, Shaiva saint and psalmist. Copper. 21 in.
11-13 c. Polonnāruva, Ceylon. Colombo Museum.
49. Hanuman, standing on pedestal. (Monkey hero.) Copper.
21 in. 10-13 c. Ceylon. Victoria and Albert Museum, Crown
Copyright.

52. Shiva as cosmic dancer (detail of Figure 1).

53. Tantric Buddhist-Hindū Purusha and Shakti. Brass. 16 c.
Nepāl. Formerly G. Chowne.
54. Bodhisattva (?). Brass. 16 c. Nepāl. Calcutta School of Art.
55. Trampled dwarf, with attributes of Shiva (part of 53).

56. Trimūrti (Trinity) seated figure. Copper gilt. 14-15 c. Nepāl.
Calcutta School of Art.

57. Avalokiteshvara (Padmapāni). Copper gilt, jewelled. 9 c.
Nepāl. 12⅜ in. Museum of Fine Arts, Boston.

58. Krishna with flute. Brass. Gūjarāt. 16-17 c. 9 in. Museum of
Fine Arts, Boston.

59. Hanuman. Copper. 16-17 c. So. India. British Museum.

CHAPTER SECOND   SCULPTURE

INDIAN SCULPTURE, WHICH EXISTS
in bewildering variety and quantity, has never been
systematically studied.   For want of space we shall
not attempt here anything like a detailed history, but
rather take certain leading types and endeavour to
investigate their psychology and to describe their
main stylistic peculiarities.

At the outset we are faced with a problem which
arises also in connection with the architecture, viz.,
the lack of evidence regarding the origins of an art
that is already highly evolved when we meet with
its first monuments in stone.   The solution, as in the
case of architecture, is to be found in the early use
of impermanent materials—clay, stucco, wood: and
also, perhaps, in the destruction of images made in
precious metal, like the golden image of Sītā mentioned in the *Rāmāyana*.   Abundant references and
remains exist to show that such perishable materials
were continuously made use of from the beginning
up to modern times; for example, temporary images
of mud are made at the present day, such as the great
figure of Bhīma at Benares, annually swept away by
the Ganges floods and annually renewed; or, again,
the painted mud images made for *bali* ceremonies in
Ceylon.   Analogous also to these survivals are children's dolls (even the realistic terra-cotta figures of

Lucknow), puppet-shows, and actors' masks.

Early Buddhism, as we have seen, is strictly rationalistic, and could no more have inspired a metaphysical art than the debates of a modern ethical society could become poetry. The early Sūtras, indeed, expressly condemn the arts, inasmuch as "form, sound, taste, smell, touch, intoxicate beings." It is thus fairly evident that before Buddhism developed into a popular State religion (under Asoka) there can hardly have existed any "Buddhist art." But Buddha never denied the existence of the Brāhmanical gods, he merely emphasised the view that these gods formed part of the *samsāra* and stood in need of salvation as much as men ; and there is every reason to suppose that the Buddhist laity continued to follow already existing animistic cults, and to worship images of gods constructed of wood and clay.* The most remarkable monuments of the 3rd century B.C. are the stone columns on which are inscribed the famous edicts of Asoka. The capital of one of these is illustrated in fig. 17. Already in Asoka's time there is much talk of the gods ; and though there is little stone sculpture of his date, other than the magnificent capitals of his inscribed pillars, we find at Bhar-

* Hindū images were certainly in use as early as the 4th century B.C. (*Indian Antiquary*, 1909, pp. 145–149).

hut, Sānchī, and Bodh Gayā, a century later, that Buddhism had already begun to organise a theology of its own. The principal members of this early Buddhist pantheon are the Guardians of the Four Quarters, represented as beneficent *yaksha* and *nāga* kings, and the Earth Goddess, represented as a *yakshī*. These forms are carved in low relief on the sides of the stone pillars of the gateways of the railings at Bharhut (fig. 19); but there are damaged remnants of similar figures in the round from Mathurā, Besnagar, and from Patna (Pātaliputra). Another instance of sculpture in the round is afforded by the beautiful bracket figures of the Sānchī gates (figs. 19*a* and 79)—dryads, leaning outwards from the trees of their habitation, with fearless and unaffected grace. Beside these figures of gods and men, we find at Bharhut and Sānchī a quantity of narrative sculpture illustrating the Jātakas and episodes in the last life of Buddha; these scenes are represented on carved medallions at Bharhut, and on the gateway pillars at Sānchī. There are also fine seals from Ceylon (fig. 16) and Bhītā (fig. 18); the latter, a terra-cotta impression, probably from an ivory die, resembles in design many of the railing medallions, but is of much finer workmanship. It is remarkable that the figure of Buddha is never indicated, but he is represented only by symbols such as the slippers, umbrella, or sacred tree.

The characteristics of this Early Buddhist style are the complete naturalism of its design, with a distinct element of sensuousness, its wood-carving technique, and the general absence of foreign influences, except in a few details. The representation of animals is excellent, but inferior to that in the Asokan sculpture of a century earlier.

The art of the Amarāvatī railing (figs. 22, 23) of the 2nd century A.D. (thus about 250 years later than Sānchī) is a logical development of the earlier style of Barhut and Sānchī, and so good that it was once held to mark "the culmination of the art of sculpture in India" (Fergusson). It offers "delightful studies of animal life, combined with extremely beautiful conventionalised ornament," and "the most varied and difficult movements of the human figure are drawn and modelled with great freedom and skill" (Havell). The well-known examples on the British Museum stairs suffer from the lack of the painted plaster surface which must once have covered the stone foundation. Most of the sculpture is still in low relief on medallions, plinth, and coping ; over 16,000 square feet must once have been covered with sculptured reliefs. If there are any Hellenistic elements recog-

is no northern work of equal rank, though others in Ceylon are nearly as good. A nearer approach to the gracious movement of the classic type of Indian sculpture is found in some of the sculptured *dwāra-pālas*, the *nāga* door-guardians of the entrances to the Anurādhapura vihāras (fig. 25). Animal processions are represented on the beautiful carved moonstone doorsteps, a form recalling the half-medallions of the Indian railings. A relief at Isurumuniya (fig. 26) resembles the love scenes of the Ajantā paintings. The Gupta style in continental India is likewise characterised by the suavity and fulness of its forms, and its closely clinging transparent draperies. The best examples are from Sārnāth (fig. 24) and Mathurā; the inscribed Buddha from Mānkuwar; the bronze figures from Sultānganj (Bengal) and Buddhavāni (Kistna dist.) (fig. 3); and the cave sculptures from Besnagar (Bhopal), Ajantā, Bādāmī, and elsewhere. The beautiful Vadrāntapa seal, which may be dated on palæographic grounds about 600, has details very like contemporary work at Ajantā, but the figure shows advanced tendencies in its very slender waist. It is possible that the Ceylon bronze figure of Pattini (British Museum), in which the slender waist is also much emphasised, is also as early as the 7th century.

We have so far left unmentioned the Græco-

52

SCULPTURE

Buddhist sculpture of the first three centuries after Christ, from Gandhāra in Afghanistān and Mathurā and Sārnāth in India : partly because the former group belongs more to the history of Central Asian than of Indian art, and partly because by the close of the 4th century practically all trace of Græco-Roman influences has disappeared in India,* even in the north, so that the Græco-Buddhist sculpture as a whole is of small importance in the history of Indian art, except for iconography. In the latter sense, however, it is very important, because its rise nearly coincides with the first representation† of Buddha otherwise than by symbols, and with the full development of the Mahāyāna Buddhist pantheon in all its main outlines. Gandhāra sculpture is the work of Græco-Roman craftsmen or Indian imitators, working for Indo-Scythian kings who patronised Buddhism as a State religion; it is a thoroughly hybrid art in which provincial Roman forms are adapted to the purposes of Indian imagery. Thus we find Apollo as the proto-

* As even Mr Vincent Smith admits (*History of Fine Art in India and Ceylon*, p. 390) : "Whatever influence Greece had exercised on Indian art was practically exhausted by A.D. 400."

† There can be little doubt that Buddha images existed before the Gandhāra sculptures. See Burgess, *Journal of Indian Art*, vol. viii. p. 33, and Sister Nivedita, *Modern Review* (Calcutta), July, August 1910.

type of Buddha, posing in the attitude of an Indian *yogī*, while other god-forms are taken over with even less modification. The æsthetic merits of this purely commercial art are of the same order with, but scarcely equal to, those of modern Catholic plaster saints; it is as far removed from the great Greek art that lies behind it, as from the classic Indian art of several centuries later. Figs. 20, 21 represent one of the best examples of the Gandhāra seated Buddhas, and a characteristic Bodhisattva; both above the average in merit, and distinguished by a certain dignity and somewhat effeminate grace.

Before considering examples of the classic phase of Indian sculpture in the 7th and 8th centuries, and its survivals and developments in later mediæval works, let us briefly consider it as a whole. This art, as Maindron remarks, has been judged by most writers " with an injustice for which the only excuse appears to be its extraordinary naïveté, when it is not the result of a pious bigotry as exaggerated as that of the conquering Musulmāns." It has indeed only been judged by special standards quite unconnected with the law of its growth or the growth of any art of like kind.

Those who regard the terra-cotta statuettes of Lucknow as the " very highest form of fine art in

India "—who are unable, in their study of "influen-ces," to distinguish external form from informing spirit—who believe in a "progress" of art from Giot-to to Raphael—and those who consider their own the only true vision of God—certainly none of these are likely to praise the classic Mahāyāna Buddhist or Brāhmanical art. But those who have learnt the language of Giotto, or have understood the imagers of Chartres, or in whom the earliest Egyptian and archaic Greek sculpture has awakened the fear of beauty—these the classic art of India will also move.

There are tests more universal than those of par-ticular canons or personal likes and dislikes. A great art expresses a clear and impassioned vision of life: each unessential statement detracts from its power. A purely æsthetic standard is given by Leonardo da Vinci—"That figure is most worthy of praise which by its action best expresses the passion that animates it." There is no going behind this to con-nect the goodness or badness of the work of art with the supposed goodness or badness of the informing passion. It is no essential business of art to incite to good or bad actions, and nearly all art which has any such conscious purpose is sentimental. The true eth-ical value of art appears in its quality of detachment and vision. This is brought out most clearly in the

great text of Hsieh Ho (Chinese, 6th century)—
"Whether or not the work exhibits the fusion of the
rhythm of the spirit with the movement of living
things." We may note in passing that this thought
most likely derives from Indian philosophy: trans-
lated back into Indian, it would run—"Whether or
not the work reveals the Self (*ātman*) within the
form (*rūpa*)." Practically the same test is laid down
by a modern critic (C. J. Holmes) in demanding in
a great work of art the qualities of Unity, Vitality,
Infinity, Repose ; for these are no more or less than
the rhythms or economy of the spirit. The presence
of this spirit is Beauty.

A confusion of two different things is often made
in speaking of the subject-matter of art. It is often
rightly said, both that the subject-matter is of small
importance, and that the subject-matter of great art
is always the same. In the first case, it is the immediate or apparent subject-matter—the representative element—that is spoken of ; it is here that we
feel personal likes and dislikes. To be guided by
such likes and dislikes is always right for a practis-
ing artist and for all those who do not desire a cosmo-
politan experience ; and indeed, to be a connoisseur
and perfectly dispassionate critic of many arts or religions is rarely compatible with impassioned devo-

tion to a single one. It may be freely granted that in a self-contained community where art is flourishing, ignorance of other arts is not a proof of lack of cultivation. It matters not that the imagers of Chartres knew nothing of archaic Greek; the spirit in them was the same. But it argues a terrible degree of callousness that those whose world is so much larger, and especially those who actually travel or spend the greater part of their life in India, should make no effort to understand her life and art. This, for them, is lack of cultivation. I do not ask for more scholasticism, but for more imagination; for without this, all that can be accomplished in India, by foreigners or by Indians, must be vandalism.

I do not perceive a fundamental distinction of arts as national—Indian, Greek, or English. All art interprets life; it is like the *Vedas*, eternal, independent of the accidental conditions of those who see or hear. Hence, if one should say that he is touched by the Italian, and not by the Chinese primitives, or by Greek, and not by Egyptian or Indian sculpture, we understand that he has done no more than accept a formula. It is this habit of accepting formulas which makes it so often possible for one form of truth to be used in denial of all others; like Michael Angelo, we are apt to say that Italian painting is good, and therefore good painting is Italian. This not only prevents our understanding the arts of other races, but is the chief cause of the neglect of living artists: patrons are not sufficiently sensitive to trust their judgment outside the accepted formulas.

To cultivate same-sightedness, to recognise one reality behind the pleasant and unpleasant Names and Forms, the familiar and unfamiliar formulas, it is needful to go behind the merely representative element to the purely emotional content of art, its dealings with love and death, for these

> "are exactly the same to all in all nations and times
>   all over the earth."

It is this content, the movement of the spirit, that is the universal subject-matter of art.

We ought not, then, to like a work of art merely because it is like something we like. It is unworthy to exploit a picture or a phrase merely as a substitute for a beautiful environment or a beloved friend. We ought not to demand to be pleased and flattered, for our true need is to be touched by love or fear. The meaning of art is far deeper than that of its immediate subject.

The immediate subject, however, is well worthy our close study when it is hieratic or mythological, that is whenever it represents racial types rather than

58

individuals. For the gods are the dreams of the race, in whom its intentions are most perfectly fulfilled. From them we come to know its innermost desires and purposes. These dreams are the guardians —*dharmapālas*—of the group, shaped and reshaped by itself subconsciously for the guidance of every one of its children. It must thus be an idle thing to speak of a love of India, which does not imply a love of her gods and heroes. Above all is this true for Indians: he is no longer an Indian, whatever his birth, who can stand before the Trimūrti at Elephanta, not saying "But so did I will it! So shall I will it." Not only for Indians, however; for this Indian art of the 7th or 8th century is not merely an Indian dream, but also a dream of humanity—humanity that sooner or later will acknowledge in the same words the significance of all great art. It will be perceived that the world-will has nowhere utterly failed of its purpose: and he will be no citizen of the future world who regards any one of its clear expressions as meaningless for him.

That which is rarest and most universal in the classic Indian art is its supreme transparency. I cannot think of any works in which the movement of the spirit shines more radiantly than in such images as the Elūra Shiva (fig. 30) or the Avalokiteshvara

59

of Ceylon (fig. 28). Their gesture seems to express an eternal youth; such a shape is theirs, as some most ancient and gracious spirit might assume, vouchsafing vision to a worshipper. And it is the same all-embracing vision that appears in the most awful and tamasic forms; in this art Bhairava was not yet repulsive, nor Kālī ugly. Those who had this vision saw one Protean life behind all Names and Forms— they worshipped Death and Life alike, for they knew that That which pervades this universe is changeless and imperishable,

> " Its seat of dalliance men may see,
> Itself no man beholdeth."

Perceiving this, how could sensuous loveliness bind them fast, or terror affright them? Thus they were not afraid either of Love or Death, but played their part without dismay or elation; and this Freedom is the secret of the power in their art.

Because of its freedom, we must not suppose that this art obeyed only unwritten laws: on the contrary, there is every reason to believe that those exact rules which are usually supposed to fetter inspiration were very implicitly obeyed. We know that in Japan the most apparently spontaneous work was the product of a very minute and highly formalised technique; and perhaps it is always just the most profound inspiration which not only can utilise, but demands precise formulas—

"Ideas cannot be given but in their minutely appropriate words, nor can a design be made without its minutely appropriate execution."

The conscious concrete ideal, the canon, of the *Shilpashāstras*, to which Sukrāchārya refers, first forbids such anatomical statements as are irrelevant for the artist's purpose, and secondly, tabulates in a very convenient manner the proportions of an ideal figure, or, more strictly speaking, several sets of such proportions according to the kind of figure to be made. An account of one must suffice, the "nine-face" system used for most images of gods. Here the face (from the chin to the roots of the hair) is taken as the unit, the height of an ideal figure being nine times as much: the trunk is three such units, the thigh and shank two each, while the neck, knee, and height of the ankle complete another. The hands and feet are each one unit in length. The measurements go into much greater detail, useful only for colossal figures, for the construction of which a very ingenious system of plumb-lines was devised. The net result of all these written and unwritten rules is that the typical figure has broad shoulders and a slender waist (like a lion), smooth limbs, tapering and slender fing-

61

ers, long arms, a deep navel, and large and long eyes. These ideals are also closely approached in the finest type of living figure, such as one may see every day on the *ghāts* at Trivenī or Benares.

There is one peculiarity of Hindū and Mahāyāna Buddhist art which has excited the resentment of many, and is apt to distract even the discerning. This is the representation, in certain types, of figures with four or more arms and two or more faces (*e.g.* figs. 1, 34*a*, 40, 50, 54, 56, 66 in this work). It should suffice to point out that such combinations, whether of complex human forms, or of human and winged or animal forms, have been used by the greatest artists of all ages. If such conventions are intrinsically bad art, then with the Indian works are equally condemned the Egyptian Sphinx, the Grecian Nike, and the Mediæval angels—to say nothing of modern works such as Rodin's "Centaur." In truth, however, the good and bad in a collection of Indian images are to be distinguished in more subtle ways than by a mere counting of arms. Such constructions are only faults when they no longer facilitate the expression of life.

It is characteristic of Indian sculpture almost throughout that its forms are healthy. The ascetic is indeed represented as emaciated: but the shapes of the gods afford abundant evidence of constant delight in the firmness and smoothness of flesh. This voluptuousness becomes most impressive in the most spiritual works; for these combine all the slender elegance and spiritual grace of Gothic with the fullest possible development of physical forms—

"The more abstract the truth you wish to teach, the more must you allure the senses to it."

Even in the best of Gothic art there are traces of a conflict, a duality of soul and body. If in many works of ancient Greece there is no such conflict, this is because the body alone is presented: but in the best of the Indian sculpture flesh and spirit are inseparable. A true æsthetic monism, like a perfected morality, does not distinguish form from matter, or motive from action.

In nearly all Indian art there runs a vein of deep sex-mysticism. Not merely are female forms felt to be equally appropriate with male to adumbrate the majesty of the Over-soul, but the interplay of all psychic and physical sexual forces is felt in itself to be religious. Already we find in one of the earliest *Upanishads,*

"For just as one who dallies with a beloved wife has no consciousness of outer and inner, so the spirit also, dallying with the Self-whose-essence-is-knowledge, has no consciousness of outer and inner."

63

Here is no thought that passion is degrading—as some Christian and Buddhist monks and many modern feminists have regarded it,—but a frank recognition of the close analogy between amorous and religious ecstasy. How rich and varied must have been the emotional experience of a society to which life could appear so perfectly transparent, and where at the same time the most austere asceticism was a beloved ideal for all those who sought to pass over life's Wandering! It is thus that the imager, speaking always for the race, rather than of personal idiosyncrasies, set side by side on his cathedral walls the *yogī* and the *apsarā*, the saint and the ideal courtesan; accepting life as he saw it, he interpreted all its phenomena with perfect catholicity of vision. Perhaps for Western readers the best introduction to such Indian modes of thought is to be found in the writings of William Blake, who in one and the same poem could write

> " Never, never I return,
> Still for victory I burn,"

and

> " Let us agree to give up love
> And root up the infernal grove."

He, in his day, could have said with the Bengālī poet of our own, that "what I have seen is unsurpassable," regarding with equal enthusiasm the Path of Pursuit and the Path of Return,—Affirmation and Denial.

The Indian sex-symbolism assumes two main forms, the recognition of which will assist the student of art: first, the desire and union of individuals, sacramental in its likeness to the union of the individual soul with God,—this is the love of the herd-girls for Krishna; and second, the creation of the world, manifestation, *līlā*, as the fruit of the union of male and female cosmic principles—*purusha* and *shakti*.

The beautiful erotic art of Konārak clearly signifies the quickening power of the Sun, perhaps not without an element of sympathetic magic. Popular explanations of such figures are scarcely less absurd than the strictures of those who condemn them from the standpoint of modern conventional propriety. They appear in Indian temple sculpture, now rarely, now frequently, simply because voluptuous ecstasy has also its due place in life; and those who interpreted life were artists. To them such figures appeared appropriate equally for the happiness they represented and for their deeper symbolism. It is noteworthy, in this connection, that such figures, and indeed all the sculptured embroidery of Indian temples, is confined to the exterior walls of the shrine, which is absolutely plain within : such is the veil of Nature, empirical life, enshrining One, not contracted or identified into variety. Those to whom all such symbols drawn from life itself appeared natural and right, would have shrunk in disgust from the more opaque erotic art of modern European salons.

While Gupta art is mainly Buddhist, the classic period is also that of the Hindū renaissance. For a time the two so closely related faiths were represented side by side, and thereafter, outside Bengal, Nepāl, and Ceylon, only the Brāhmanical forms prevail. The same Gupta art which developed into Indian classic, was the dynamic factor in the formation of the Tang Buddhist sculpture of China, and the Nara painting of Japan, as well as of the great monuments of Jāva. Thus not merely in India, but throughout Eastern Asia, the 7th and 8th centuries were ages of intense and widespread æsthetic activity, of which the seeds had been sown in India of the 5th and 6th centuries.

From these digressions let us return to the actual art.

The most typical examples of the classic sculpture are from Elūra, Māmallapuram, Ceylon, and Jāva. One of the finest of these is the rock-cut Kapila at Anurādhapura (fig. 31), beside the Isurumuniya *vihāra* : the sage is represented as a man of supreme dignity, seated in the " pose of kingly ease," gazing outwards from his cave, as if on the watch for the coming of the sons of Sāgara; this outwardly directed interest reminds us that this is the figure of a man, and no god, without detracting from its supreme grandeur.

Quite as large in design, but more spiritual, is the little Avalokiteshvara (Buddhist Saviour), also from Ceylon (fig. 28). This figure, so wise and so eternally young, is treated with complete simplicity and graciousness: the right hand is raised in the mode of teaching, the crown and ribbon are symbols of his divine rank, and the seated figure in the crown represents the Dhyāni Buddha from whom the Bodhisattva emanates as one of his many modes.

A great contrast in subject, but scarcely less impressive as a work of most consummate craftsmanship, is the very material figure of Jambhala or Kuvera, god of wealth (fig. 29), with his mongoose and money-pots, also from Ceylon and probably contemporary with the Avalokiteshvara. This Jambhala, so plump and firm and cheerful, is a very proper god of trade, as trade once was: unfortunately in these days, his throne has been usurped by *rākshasas*.

The figures of Shiva and Pārvatī in a composition at Elūra (fig. 30) are very like the Ceylon Avalokiteshvara in grace of movement and smoothness of modelling: they are seated on Kailās, with Rāvana

beneath, endeavouring to root up the mountain—
Pārvatī feels a tremor, and turns to throw her arms
about her Lord, who presses down the mountain with
his foot. Another important work at Elūra in which
more violent movement is rendered with equal power,
is the very damaged *Narasimha slaying Hiranya-
kashipu*, in the cave of the Ten Avatārs.

A different kind of sculpture, most impressive in
majesty and boldness of design, is represented by
the Trimūrti at Elephanta (fig. 33); of all classic Indian sculpture the most easily accessible. The heads
of this triple image are supreme renderings of an
ethnic type that is still familiar. The suggestion of
absolute repose veiling a profound inward life is con-
veyed equally in each of the three masks, though
these are representative of carefully differentiated
types of character.

Of equal rank with this triple mask at Elephanta is
the recumbent Nārāyana at Māmallapuram (fig. 32).
Nārāyana, worshipped by Lakshmī, rests in the in-
terval between two daily creations, on the serpent
Ananta ("Infinite"): two threatening Asuras stand
to the right. At Māmallapuram, too, there is a very
spirited rendering of a battle of Durgā with the
Asuras, and many sculptures of animals of unsurpassed grandeur, tenderness, and humour.

68

SCULPTURE

All these images, without hesitation or awkwardness, or any superfluous statement, by their action perfectly express the passion that animates them. The classic art does not rapidly decline after the 8th century ; its spirit continues to inspire a number of slightly later works, while locally a fine tradition is maintained to quite a late date. The great Madras Natarāja, perhaps of the 10th century (there are others of all dates up to the present day) we have already noticed (p. 17). A smaller and less familiar copper image (fig. 34a) is of Mahisha-mardinī, Durgā slaying the demon Mahisha, of the 9th century, from Jāva, now in the Museum at Leiden: here it is seen how nobly the many arms, even of a tāmasic form, can be used to reinforce the movement of the whole figure, in a pattern of extreme subtlety. This image of an avenging goddess moves with a sadness and tenderness that are as far removed from anger as heaven from hell. It is in this isolation and detachment that such figures most fully voice the Indian theory of life: if such a text as the Chandī Parva of the Mārkandeya Purāna means but little to a Western student, an image such as this certainly reveals much of what it could mean for a Hindū. It would indeed scarcely be too much to say that the study of the art, side by side with that of *sruti* and *smriti*, is absol-

utely essential for a full understanding of Hinduism.
We shall see subsequently that this is as true of later
Vaishnava painting as of classic Shaivite sculpture.

Another Jāvanese image of great interest is the
Ganesha of fig. 36. Here we perceive that the most
bizarre motif, treated in harmony with the spirit of a
great tradition, can become expressive of profound
wisdom.

Jāva is rich in other beautiful images : one more,
selected from these, is the Dhyāni Buddha of fig. 35,
perhaps of the 9th century. The most striking of the
Jāvanese sculptures, however, are not the single
works, but the long series of reliefs which line the
procession paths (extending for nearly two miles) of
the great Buddhist monument at Borōbodur. These
sculptures illustrate, not a complex mythology, but
the simple events of the *jātakas* and histories of the
life of Buddha, and are uniformly gentle in their sentiment, and suave and full in form. These beautiful reliefs are by far the best of Indian sculptures dealing
with events of ordinary human life, and as such offer,
perhaps, an easier introduction to Oriental art than
the more learned works. No criticism could be better
than Mr Havell's, who writes that each group and
figure is "absolutely true and sincere in expression
of face, gesture, and pose of body; and the actions

than anything in India, but still reminiscent of the great Trimūrti at Elephanta. The work in Cambodia was interrupted in the 12th century and never resumed. Burma and Siam were also Indianised at an early period, and remain Buddhist to this day. The Buddhist art of China derived at first from Bactria through Turkestan, afterwards (4th century) directly from India, and maintained a hieratic tradition there and in Japan until the 14th century, when the Zen thought gave to Buddhist art a new impulse.

We can now return to India, and study the mediæval sculpture, of which some is still Buddhist, but the greater part Hindū. One of the most important groups is that of the southern Shaivite bronzes, including the Natarāja (figs. 1 and 52) already described, and many later examples. A number of these represent the great Tamil saints of the centuries preceding the 10th, Mānikka Vāçagar (fig. 47), Apparswāmi, Sundara Mūrti Swāmi (fig. 48), Tiru Jñāna Sambandha Swāmi; fine examples of these have been found at Polonnāruva. A figure of Hanuman, from Ceylon (fig. 49), now at South Kensington, is strangely touching in its combination of semi-divine intelligence with animal devotion and irrepressible vitality; he wears a gravity not altogether incompatible with mischievous adventure. With these should perhaps be grouped the beautiful figure of a sage, at Polonnāruva, miscalled a likeness of Parākrama Bāhu the Great (fig. 34); it may well be earlier.

About three centuries later are the very beautiful brass portrait figures of Krishnarāya of Vijayanagar and his queens (1510–1529 A.D.) (fig. 51). Dravidian sculpture in stone, most often as part of the great monolithic pillars of the "thousand pillared halls," continues to flourish up to the end of the 17th century; but the later work, though very highly finished, often lacks tenderness and aims rather to express a demoniac power.

In the north we meet with much excellent Buddhist sculpture of the classic and later periods in Behar and Bengal, including a number of as yet little known bronzes. The gracious head of Tārā (*shakti* of Avalokiteshvara) from Sārnāth (fig. 40) belongs to the best type of mediæval Buddhist sculpture under the Pāla kings of Bengal. A fragment (fig. 39) preserved at Gwaliar is but one of the many beautiful images of youthful women that the mediæval art affords. Two headless figures from Sārnāth (figs. 41, 42) admirably illustrate ideal Kshatriya and Brāhman types.

The Buddhist tradition has survived in Nepāl to the present day, showing marked decadence only perhaps in the last century. From Nepāl it passed with slight modification to Tibet. Many works in Indian and European collections are regarded as Tibetan, but are properly of Nepalese origin, and even the truly Tibetan works are mostly due to the activity of Nepalese craftsmen settled near Lhasa. Early and very fine Nepalese works are still frequently met with. The standing Avalokiteshvara (fig. 57), reminiscent of the painted Bodhisattva at Ajantā (fig. 60), is perhaps older than the 12th century. The Calcutta school of art collection is rich in fine examples, of which a Trimūrti (fig. 56) and a Bodhisattva (?) (fig. 54) are illustrated here. One of a pair of beautiful and gracious hands is reproduced in fig. 5. Figs. 53 and 55 are details from one of the dual images, in which the close connection, almost identity, of Tāntric Buddhist with Shaivite art, is clearly exhibited; the embracing figures are essentially those of Shiva and Pārvatī, or more generally, Purusha and Shakti, while the trampled dwarf (who has himself the attributes of the Shiva by whose foot he is destroyed) we have already seen (fig. 1) to be an old Hindū motif. It is noteworthy that the Nepalese imagers also occasionally rendered Vaishnava subjects, such as Vishnu, or Krishna and Rādhā.

Much of the best mediæval Hindū sculpture is

from Orissa. It would be hard to find anywhere in the world a more perfect example of the adaptation of sculpture to architecture, than is afforded by the temple of the Sun at Konārak. It is remarkable how like are the façades of these Orissan cathedrals, their statues inseparable from the framework of the building itself, to the contemporary churches of Western Europe; without, of course, any possible direct connections. It is one of those many examples where like requirements and intentions have stimulated the discovery of similar principles of craftsmanship. The best Konārak figures are characterised by an exquisite smoothness and vitality. The sculptures of women are frankly the work of lovers (figs. 43, 44). But it is perhaps the animals that are most impressive; the *Led Horse* (fig. 46) is of unsurpassed grandeur; some of the smaller horses drawing the temple on its huge wheels, express a mood of sadness almost as profound as that of the Jāvanese Mahisha-mardinī. There is an important group of a *Guru and Disciples* in the Indian Museum at South Kensington, formerly miscalled Nepalese, but almost certainly from Konārak.

In Ceylon the hieratic sculpture in metal, stone, or brick rapidly declines after the 14th century or even earlier; in the 18th only its formal traditions survive, but even the most awkward of the later works according to the canon, are preferable to the lifeless alabaster images now frequently imported from Burma. On the other hand, some of the mediæval and more recent wooden images and modern Sinhalese *bali*-figures and devil-dancers' masks retain the spirit of much earlier work and merit careful study.

Good examples of mediæval wood sculpture are shown in fig. 45, representing the South Indian and Ceylonese goddess Pattinī (a manifestation of Pārvatī), and her husband, or perhaps a nāga king. A date as early as the 11th century has been suggested for these.*

In Madras and Tanjore there are still skilful imagers and founders as well as learned architects. Certain copper figures recently produced are probably as good as any of the last two centuries.

In northern India there is little modern work of high value. A flourishing school of craftsmen in Jaipur produces creditable images of Hindū gods in white marble, greatly in demand throughout Hindustān. One living Jaipur artist, Māli Rām, deserves mention for his excellent workmanship in stone, wood, and metal, ranging from engraved seals to large marble images and metal masks. The realistic terra-cotta images

* Parker, *Ancient Ceylon*, p. 631.

SCULPTURE

of Lucknow are remarkable only for the modeller's skill in photographic reproduction, with a decided preference for diseased and famine-stricken subjects. The school of art style of Bombay is pseudo-Parisian. The work of the Calcutta school in sculpture is less interesting than the painting.

Seal of the Court of Vadrāntapa, 6th century A.D., representing Gaja-Lakshmī.   Indian Museum, S. Kensington.

60. A Bodhisattva, Ajantā. 5-6 c. Fresco. Cave 1.

61. 62. Details from Ajantā. Head of a girl. Ajantā fresco. Cave
17, tracing. Girl seated, Ajantā fresco. Cave 1, tracing.
63. Elephant. Ajantā. Cave 17. (*Chhadanta Jātaka*).
64. Princess with lotus flower. Rock pocket at Sīgiriya, Ceylon.
5 c. Fresco.

65. Buddha quells the mad elephant (Airavatī). Nepāl. Palm-
leaf MS. 1½ in. 14-15 c.
66. Tārā (compassionate). Wooden covers of MS. 2 in. Nepāl.
67. Episode from *Vessantara Jātaka* (copied). Abt. 22 in. Tem-
pera. On Degaldoruwa Vihāra wall, near Kandy, Ceylon.
68. *Pichcha-mal* (jessamine) decoration. Wooden covers of MS.
Kandy, Ceylon.

69. Death of Bhīshma. Painting on paper. Rājput. 16 c. 3 x 6 in.
Freer Gallery of Art, Washington, D. C.
70. Kālīya-damana, Krishna quelling the serpent demon (*nāga*).
Painted on paper. Rājput. 18 c. 10 x 7 in. Metropolitan
Museum of Art, New York.

71. Head of a girl singing. Paper cartoon (part of the cartoon). Jaipur. Rājput. 18 c. 13½ in. Metropolitan Museum of Art, New York.

72. Krishna dancing. Paper cartoon. Jaipur. Rājput. 18 c. Museum of Fine Arts, Boston.

73. Portrait of a woman. Brush drawing on paper. 4 in. 18-19 c. Fogg Museum, Cambridge.

74. Chorus of musicians and dancers for Krishna. Unfinished painting on paper. Rājput (Pahārī). 18 c. 3¼ x 4 in. Museum of Fine Arts, Boston.

75. Rāma, Sītā, and Lakshman. Painted on paper. Rājput (Pahārī). 17-18 c. 8 in. Formerly the author's, now lost.
76. Shiva and Pārvatī. Unfinished painting. Rājput (Pahārī). 18 c. 7¾ x 6 in. Author.
77. Shiva and Pārvatī. Painting on paper. Rājput (Pahārī). 19 c. 9 x 6 in. Museum of Fine Arts, Boston.
78. Rāginī Torī (musical mode). Painted on paper. Rājput (Jaipur), 8 x 5 in. Calcutta School of Art.

79. Gateway (*torana*). Sandstone *stūpa* at Sāñchī. 2 c., B.C.

PAINTINGS ARE EASILY DESTROYED
by natural causes or deliberate injuries; and what
remains of Indian painting cannot be the hundredth
or even the thousandth part of what once existed.
We cannot, however, doubt that the art was continuously practised from pre-Buddhist times to the present day. Frescoes (*patibhāna cittam*, or "conversation pictures," *i.e.* love scenes) are mentioned in
the oldest Pāli literature: these were condemned by
Buddha, who permitted only the representation of
"wreaths and creepers." A picture gallery (*cittāgāra*)
belonging to King Pasenadi of Kosala is also referred
to. The Bharhut sculptures imply the existence of a
contemporary school of painting, and actual remains
of the 2nd or 1st century B.C. exist in caves at Rām-
garh in Orissa. At Ajantā, however, there exists a
far more important series of paintings, executed on
the walls of the excavated vihāras, ranging from the
1st to the middle of the 7th century A.D. Thus, many
of the best works are of the Gupta period, while the
latest, in Caves I. and XVII., fall just within the
classic age. There are also paintings of the 6th century at Bāgh in Mālwā, and of the 5th at Sīgiri in
Ceylon. From 650 to 1550 A.D. there survive no
remains of Indian painting, except a few Nepālese
Buddhist miniatures and some fragments in Ceylon.

After 1550 we are able to pick up once more the thread of the old traditions, in the Rājput painting of Rājputāna and the Panjāb Himālayas, the book-covers of Orissan MSS., and popular and hieratic wall painting in all parts of India and Ceylon; while there also appears the new eclectic style of the Mughals.

The paintings of Ajantā, though much damaged, still form the greatest extant monument of ancient painting and the only school except Egyptian in which a dark-skinned race is taken as the normal type. One does not know whether to wonder most at their advanced technique, or at the emotional intensity that informs these works, as if with a life very near our own—for they are as modern in their draughtmanship as in sentiment. They belong to the same courtly-religious culture as that which finds expression in the works of Kālidāsa, and show the same deep understanding of the hearts of men and women and animals that has given to Shakuntalā her immortality, and shines even through the artificialities of Bāna.

The Ajantā art, though it deals with religious subjects, is too free to be spoken of as hieratic; it is rather discovering than following the types that were to remain prepotent through so many later centuries. The gracious movement, the serene self-possession

82

PAINTING

of these noble figures, the love that enfolds their every gesture, their profound sadness even in moments of greatest joy—as if all their laughter were near to tears—produce an impression never to be forgotten in the mind of one who stands for the first time in these dark halls thus hung with painted tapestry. This is a profoundly cultivated art; everywhere touched by ardour and tenderness, but expressing these deepest feelings of distress or gladness within the limits of a life of closely regulated etiquette. So deeply emotional it is, that this reserve is an essential part of it; passion and shyness are inseparable qualities. Never in the world was any art less sentimental.

The life depicted is that of earthly or heavenly courts and palaces; there is no such transfiguration of the everyday life of villages and forests as appears in the Rājput works; but the kings and queens, or gods and goddesses, are here endowed with such affections and sincerity, such childlike simplicity and dignity, as it is no longer easy for us to associate with the life of courts and modern aristocracies. No doubt that then (as up to the present day, wherever the past conditions survive) the peasant was himself an aristocrat, and spoke as elegantly as the courtier; but here there is a greater miracle, for we are reminded that beneath the forms of etiquette and cultivation,

83

the movement of the spirit may be as sure and swift as in any more naïve culture of the folk. It is not only the poor, but also the rich, that are fit for the kingdom of heaven, are indeed the greatest in heaven. This is finer and greater than any democratic theory of equality; a condition where the most and the least cultivated share in a common courtesy, and kings and peasants are equally contented and unabashed. Perhaps this ideal of aristocracy also existed in 13th-century Europe; at least, to find a parallel in Western art, for these movements of ardour and tenderness, one must go back to Chartres and the Italian primitives, with whom, indeed, the Indian artists have always so much in common.

The *Chhadanta Jātaka*, or Birth-story of the Six-tusked Elephant, is one the most beautiful of all Buddhist legends: but the painting, in Cave XVII., tells it with a grief more poignant than any words, and a most profound realisation of the untold suffering that is the fruit of ill-will. On one side stands the great white elephant (fig. 63), an incarnation of him who was to become the Buddha—of whom it is said that there is no spot on earth where he has not sacrificed his body for the sake of creatures—towering like a snowy mountain above the hunter, for whom he cuts away his own tusks. Upon the

84

other side, in a pavilion, lies the young queen who had once been the Bodhisattva's wife—offended at a little thing, and now seeking her revenge. She is very young, and gentle and tender-hearted, and sends her hunters out to bring these tusks for her (she cannot be happy without them), as lightly as the modern woman sends her emissaries into the equatorial forests and the polar wastes to bring her back the spoils of death. She is full of impatience for the hunters to return; but when the successful one comes back at last, bringing the tokens of him whom she knew in her heart to be the noblest of all living things, then she is not glad, but is crushed by such overwhelming grief that it breaks her child's heart and ends her life.

The great figure in Cave I. (fig. 60) probably represents the Bodhisattva Avalokiteshvara,* or possibly the departure of Prince Siddhārtha from his palace ("The Great Renunciation"). In either case, its motif is that of a great Being turning away from all attachments to seek a cure for the world's sorrow. These figures are treated with the same supreme command of gesture and largeness of design that we find in the best of the 8th-century sculpture. It seems,

* The rocky background perhaps indicating Mt. Potalaka; the chief female figure a *shakti*.

indeed, as if the full development of painting a little preceded that of the finest sculpture.

We know from literary references that portrait painting, though expressly condemned in connection with religious art, was an admired accomplishment practised by princes and others, and even by women. And amongst the Ajantā figures there are some which we cannot but regard as portraits, or which at least could very well be portraits. But these, as we should expect, are portraits in the old Asiatic sense, not to be judged by the accuracy of their likeness to an individual at one particular moment, but as expressing the character of an age; for it is this character, and not the mere peculiarities, which the great artist perceives through love and insight in every individual whom he studies. Perhaps there could not anywhere be found a more expressive rendering of the mystery of woman, or a more intimate revelation of a sensuous and sensitive nature, than in the Ajantā fragment of which the outlines are reproduced in fig. 61 ; and some others like it, from the great "*Ceylon Battle*." Some such portrait as this, King Dushyanta had of Shakuntalā:

"A graceful arch of brows above great eyes."

The technique of all these works is of great interest for the student of the materials of the painter's craft and the history of painting. The wall was prepared by applying a mixture of clay, cow-dung and pulverised trap-rock, sometimes also mixed with rice-husks, to the rough excavated surface of the rock. This first layer of $\frac{1}{8}$ to $\frac{3}{4}$ inch was overlaid with a skin of fine white polished plaster, covering also the whole interior of the cave, including the sculptures. The process of painting (to argue back from modern practice in India) differed chiefly from Italian fresco in the greater length of time the Indian lime remains damp, and in the fact that the surface, after colouring, is burnished with a small trowel, by which process the colour is deeply ingrained. The first brush work is "a bold red line drawing on the white plaster ... next comes a thinnish terra-verde monochrome, showing some of the red through it; then the local colour; then a strengthening of the outlines with blacks and browns, giving great decision, but also a certain flatness; last a little shading if necessary" (Herringham). Perhaps the most noteworthy technical peculiarity of the work at Ajantā is that it is essentially an art of brush drawing, depending for its expression mainly on the power and swiftness of its outlines and not at all on any attempt at producing an illusion of relief. The most difficult problems of perspective are attacked with reckless courage (fig. 62).

There are many quite distinct styles of drawing of which the relations and history have never been adequately studied.

At Sīgiri in Ceylon there are a few paintings of the 5th century in a style very near to Ajantā, representing half figures of queens or goddesses (fig. 64) with servants carrying flowers. The basis and technique are also practically the same as at Ajantā.

We know very little of mediæval Buddhist painting from actual Indian remains. We have only the painted covers and illustrations of a few Nepalese MS. (figs. 65, 66). Wall-paintings, perhaps of the 12th century, have been found at Polonnāruva in Ceylon.

It will be seen that by a fortunate chance we are fairly well acquainted with the courtly Buddhist painting of the Gupta and early classic period; though the art seems to be still developing, and perhaps even finer work has been lost. But we have no remains at all of contemporary Brāhmanical art—scenes from the epics, or paintings of the *devas*, such as a Bengal king once drew with magic chalk upon his palace walls—nor of any paintings on wood or cloth: nor of the popular folk-art which must have existed side by side with the high culture. We find the traces of these, however, when we recover the indigenous tradition a thousand years later.

PAINTING

In Rājputāna and the Panjāb Himālayas we find surviving, even into the 19th century, a school of religious art which is partly hieratic and partly of folk-inspiration. In its pure forms—figs. 70, 71 may be taken as typical,—this art is essentially classic; it depends for its language upon fundamental forms and significant relations of mass and space, and for its content, upon whatever in life is universal, while it makes no study of transient expressions and individual peculiarities. Where it departs from this simplicity and seeks for the picturesque, or where it portrays individuals rather than types, we can recognise foreign influence. Thus Rājput painting contrasts in every way with the secular Mughal art with which it is largely contemporary. That secular and professional school was an affair of but two hundred years; but the hieratic and folk-art takes us back through many centuries, further even than Ajantā, to that "Early Asiatic," of which a Western phase has been preserved in the remains of ancient Crete.

In sentiment and method the Rājput art presents analogies with the contemporary music. Its chief motifs are traditional themes, upon which each artist improvised more or less freely. Thus, as in all national and long-enduring art, a tradition takes the place of individual supreme genius, but each artist

89

must exercise much more invention than mere imitation, if his works are to be, as here they were, infused with life.

Rājput painting, though not a young tradition, has all the intensity of primitive art. It is largely inspired by the impassioned Vaishnava poetry, which it so often illustrates. Its beauty is perfectly naïve, not intended to be picturesque, never sentimental, but inevitably resulting from the clear expression of deep feeling. Much of it is folk-art, drawing its imagery from the daily life of villagers and herdsmen. What the courtier would have despised is everywhere transfigured by deep love. In the contemporary Mughal art, emperors and courtiers pose for their portraits very consciously and proudly. But the herd-girls of the Pahārī drawings have eyes for none but Krishna ; the singers and the dancers are as much absorbed in their service and their art as any of those at Borōbodur : none are aware that they are overlooked. There is no more single-minded painting in the world.

The paintings fall into two groups, the *Rājasthānī*, from Rājputāna and especially Jaipur; and the *Pahārī*, or Mountain school, from the Panjāb hill-states, especially Kāngrā, Chambā, and Pūnch.

Amongst the earliest works is the *Death of Bhīsh-*

ma (fig. 69), which seems to preserve the composition characteristic of the old Buddhist *parinirvānas*. Bhīshma, revered instructor of both Pāndavas and Kurus, fought on the side of the latter, in the Great War. Weary of the slaughter, he elected at last to meet his own fate, and fell wounded by many arrows. As he lay on his bed of arrows, a divine nature possessed him ; while he lay, " expectant of his hour, resembling in splendour the setting sun, like to a fire about to go out," he expounded, before Krishna, Duryodhana and the five Pāndavas, all the duties of men of the various classes. The original drawing is of great delicacy and purity of colour. There will be seen on the left, the seven *rishis*, including Nārada with his *vīnā*; behind Bhīshma's head, Krishna, with four arms, a club, a chank and a lotus flower; then Duryodhana; and on the right, the five Pāndavas.

The *Death of Bhīshma* is probably as old as the 16th century. Most of the Rājput pictures which are well preserved belong to the 18th century, but all are difficult to date, as there is no rapid change of style, and the pictures are never signed or dated. It is much easier to separate them geographically. A typical Pahārī (Kāngrā) work of the early 18th century is the *Kālīya Damana* of fig. 70; here Krishna has overcome the hydra Kālīya, and while Nand and

Yashodā on the river bank are anxious for his safety, the hydra's beautiful wives are bending low to kiss the feet of the Lord of the World to pray for their husband's life. Here, as always in the Pahārī drawings, and the Epic and Purānic literature, "every act consumes the whole vital energy of being, every pose is the mirror of the soul in an imperious moment." * Two distinct types of movement, on water and on land, are clearly distinguished. The feminine type that these Kāngrā painters loved, so beautiful and passionate and shy, is one entirely true, and expressive of the race. We are reminded again of the Greek vases. For these Rājput painters too "ont légué au monde un rêve d'art, où la pensée artistique s'est épanchée en formules larges et générales, d'où le passager et l'accidental étaient exclus. . . Dans la vie familière elle-même jamais il ne vous presentera un homme en particulier, un individu. . . Ce sera toujours l'idée de race, l'idée d'humanité, l'idée de vie dans son ensemble que vous rencontrerez dans ses plus modestes ébauches." † Educated by such art, it is still easy to discover a like perfection and tranquillity in the features and the movements of living women of the folk, in the Panjāb and the Himālayas.

* B. P. Sitaramayya and K. Hanumantha Rao, *National Education*.
† E. Pottier, *La Peinture Industrielle chez les Grecs*.

PAINTING

In perhaps no other part of the world has the tradition of ancient art survived so late.

The picture of Rāma, Sītā, and Lakshman (fig. 75) —their forest exile—belongs to the local Pahārī school of Pūnch; a naïve simplicity and force are here, somewhat exceptionally, united with tenderness and mystery. A picture of Shiva and Pārvatī (fig. 76), as the folk imagination sees them wandering or resting in the glades of the Himālayas, and here besought by Bhagīratha (the *yogī* making *tapas* beneath) to permit the Ganges to fall to earth from the Great God's matted locks, is again a typical Pahārī (Kāngrā) drawing, with a brilliancy of colouring recalling stained glass or enamel. It is dramatic, if perhaps unconscious, symbolism that represents the God so near to, yet unseen by, his devotee. Such works are sealed with absolute conviction; those who drew thus, or painted the Divine Herdsman, were realists, knowing that in this enchanted world the sudden vision of the presence of God awaited them in every cattle-fold and forest: realists in the deepest sense, for "it is not the same tree that the fool and the wise man see."

The characteristics of the Pahārī drawing are well shown also in fig. 74, a detail from an unfinished picture. All these pictures are in scale much larger than their actual size; when greatly enlarged, their true relation to an art of wall-painting becomes at once apparent. Though most of the Pahārī works are on a small scale, the existence of a fresco school could be clearly inferred from them; and indeed, wall-painting was still practised by the same artists as those who executed the small works. Some of the latter actually show painted walls, and one, a painter at work. A coarser art of popular wall-painting and house-decoration still flourishes everywhere in India.

A later Pahārī work is another picture of Shiva and Pārvatī (fig. 77)—a night scene, the Great God watching Devī as she sleeps. It is uncertain how far the representation of night effects is original in Rājput art; they occur in some of the most provincial types (Pūnch), but are rarer in Kāngrā pictures. The subject-matter frequently requires them: and certainly the dark skies and heavy monsoon clouds, broken by flashes of lightning, or crossed by lines of white birds, must be indigenous motifs. The Shiva and Pārvatī of fig. 77 is attributed to a Hindū painter of Garhwāl, whose ancestors had worked at the Mughal court, but came originally from Rājputāna; his case is exceptional, and his name, Mola Rām, is almost the only one known of all Rājput painters.

The most striking works of the Jaipur (Rājasthānī) school are the large wall and panel paintings, of which

latter there are fine examples belonging to the Mahārāja of Jaipur, and another now belongs to the Mahārāja of Cossimbazar. The former have never been
photographed; but I have been fortunate in finding
in the bazar a number of the original cartoons, drawn
on paper and most of them pricked for pouncing.
The coloured frontispiece reproduces a *Head of
Krishna* from this series, the whole figure from another version in monochrome being shown in fig. 72.
A detail from a group of musicians (fig. 71) well illustrates the characteristic Jaipur type, which is very
distinct from that of the hills, though akin to it in
simplicity of outline and neglect of relief, akin also
in the frequent use of temperate curves, often ap-
proximating to a straight line. The complete composition from which these details are given represents a dance of Rādhā and Krishna, with a chorus
of musicians on either hand.

Portraiture is very rare amongst the Pahārī drawings; but there are numerous portraits in Rājputāna,
both large and small, of which fig. 73 is a typical
example, except that portraits of women are rarer
than those of men. Some of these reveal as much
interest in individual character as any of the Mughal
sketches; but they show less modelling, and have
simpler and more continuous outlines. The idea of

miniature and quite realistic portraiture is almost certainly of foreign origin.

There are also amongst the Jaipur works extremely beautiful sets of pictures of the *ragas* and *raginis*, or musical modes, of which an example is reproduced in fig. 78. These pictures seem to be intended to express visually the same sentiment as that which is appropriate to the mode; some, by the representation of the mode itself, personified as a minor divinity; others by the representation of a suitable scene.

Paper stencils for design in two colours, Mathurā.

To be associated with the Rājput drawings are the interesting paper stencils of Jaipur, Delhi, and Mathurā, of which examples are shown in the ac-

PAINTING

companying figures. The pictures are made on the
ground with coloured powders, as many stencils as
colours being required.

Paper stencil, Mathurā.

Beside the Rājput works, there are at least two
other noteworthy schools of Hindū painting, those of
Orissa and Tanjore. The Orissan style is known at
present only by paintings on the wooden covers of
Vaishnava MSS. of the 16th and 17th centuries. The
Tanjore style of the 18th to 19th centuries is exemplified by hieratic wall-paintings, portraits on cloth, and
books of rough sketches used by imagers and goldsmiths. The last are of special interest, on account of
the great boldness of the freehand brush outlines,
and for the extremely archaic character of some of
the designs.

The 18th-century Buddhist painting of Ceylon
appears in the narrative style of the *jātaka* paintings
on the *vihāra* walls (fig. 67); in rare illustrations of

Rāma slaying Mārīcha: Tanjore drawing.

paper MSS.; in painted wooden book-covers of palm-leaf MSS.(fig. 68); in separate panel representations of Buddha; and in the ceiling paintings, which include many fine patterns, and also representations of the " tree of life," with a festooned border, exactly in the style of the South Indian palampores. The paintings can be well studied at the Kelaniya Vihāra near Colombo, and the Degaldoruwa Vihāra near Kandy.

The latter part of the 19th century in India has been a blank, so far as any serious work in painting goes. Western influences have made fashionable the most trivial of academic realism; but not a single painter, of all those who have worked under these influences, has produced any work of permanent importance, even of its own class. The weakness of the drawing, in such works as those of Ravi Varma, and his many imitators, is only equalled by the cheapness, not to say the vulgarity, of the sentiment. The beginning of the present century has been marked by a reaction; not only in taste, leading to a renewed appreciation of the older works, but also in production, especially in Calcutta, where a group of artists led by A. N. Tagore, Vice-Principal of the School of Art, have endeavoured to recover old traditions, and give sincere expression to Indian sentiment. Their treatment of the myths has not always proved a success, mainly from lack of sufficient conviction; but they have portrayed well, though in a manner too much influenced by Japan, the delicate charm and refinement of the old Indian daily life, so far as it survives. Love, and not self-advertisement, inspires their work. Great credit is due to all such pioneers, under conditions so difficult and so hostile to sincere feeling as those which obtain in India at the present day.

Edicts, like those of Asoka, and grants are engraved on stone and metal. Sanskrit (the classic language of the Hindūs) is written in what is called the

deva-nāgarī ("city-of-the-gods") character, and nearly all vernaculars (especially Hindī) in the same, or

Two lines of a Sanskrit MS., Kāshmīr (18th or 19th century).

the same more or less modified. The nāgarī characters
are a form of the older "Bramhī" script. The complete
alphabet of forty-six letters—the only perfectly scientific alphabet ever in general use—written in Brahmī
must have been known by 500 B.C. It is based on old
Phœnician forms which probably reached India about
800 B.C. (Bühler). The old Indian MSS. are written on
birch bark, or palm leaves, the former in Kāshmīr and
the north generally, the latter in the south. Ink was already used in the 2nd century B.C., probably in the 4th,
and very possibly much earlier. Paper was not used in
India before the 10th century. Nāgarī characters are
written with a broad reed pen on the birch bark or
palm leaves, and now on paper (the oldest MS. on
paper is of the 13th century A.D.); while southern
MSS. in vernacular characters are incised with a writing style, and the incisions blackened by rubbing in
ink. From the nature of these materials, it will be
seen that but little could be done in the way of illus-

PAINTING

trating manuscripts, but the wooden covers are often painted with figure subjects or conventional decoration. The nāgarī script is monumental and severe, often very splendid in effect, but never intentionally calligraphic; the crafts of painting and writing are quite distinct.

Hamsa-pūttuva: Sinhalese drawing of the 18th century.

CHAPTER FOUR
ARCHITECTURE

80. Temple façade, excavated sanctuary (*chaitya*) at Nāsik.
About 150 B. C.

81. Rock-cut pillars, Indra Sābhā
cave. Basalt. Elūra. 9-11 c.
82. Excavated temple. Basalt.
Island of Elephanta, near
Bombay. 8 c.
83. Monolithic temple. Bhīma's
temple (*ratha*). Sandstone.
Late 7 c. Māmallapuram.

84. Bathing tank (*pokuna*) restored. Southwest view. Granulite.
5-8 c. Anurādhapura, Ceylon.

85 "Moonstone" door-step to temple or monastery. Anurādhapura,
Ceylon. 5 c. (?) Lotus centre, floral border, mythical wisdom-
birds (*hamsas*), elephants, lions, bulls, and other animals.
86. Āryāvarta temple. Sandstone. 10 c. Bhuvaneshvara.

87. Kailāsa temple, Elūra. Basalt, excavated. 8 c.

88. Pilasters and window. Detail. Subrahmaniya temple, Tanjore. 18 c.
89. *Gopuram* (tower surmounting gates of So. Indian temples). Stone and stucco. Great temple, Madurā.
90. *Mandapam* (open pillared hall) Auvadaiyar Kovil. Stone. Tanjore District. 16 c.

91. Mān Singh's palace and fort. Wholly hewn of stone, edge of vertical cliff. 15 c. Gwaliar.
92. Fort and palace. Summit of hill, half living stone, half massive masonry. 15 c. Jodhpur.
93. Ghosal Ghat, hostel for pilgrims, built by the Bhonslā rājas of Nāgpur. Sandstone. 19 c. Benares.
94. *Jhārokhā* window (balcony). 18-19 c. House near Jodhpur.

95. Interior verandah. Wood. 18 c. House at Tanjore.
96. Street architecture. Jaipur. Stone. 18-19 c.
97. Exterior verandah. House at Rāmeshwaram.
98. Interior colonnade. House at Jaffna, Ceylon.

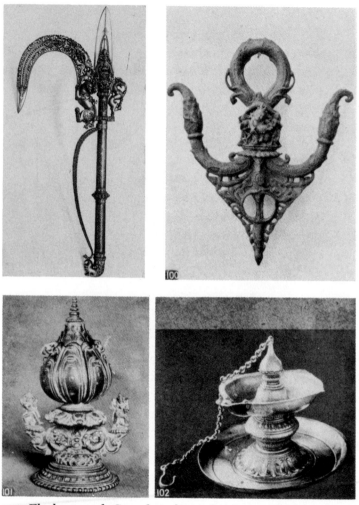

99. Elephant goad. Carved steel. 17-18 c. Louvre, Paris.
100. Architect's plummet. Bronze-coating on iron. Bengal. 6¾ in.
6 c. British Museum.
101. Lotus enclosing image of Vajra-Tārā. Bronze. 14 c. Nepāl.
Indian Museum, Calcutta.
102. *Vihāra* lamp. Silver. 18 c. Kandy. Daladā Māligāwa, Kandy,
Ceylon.

CHAPTER FOURTH ARCHITECTURE

EXCEPT IN TECHNICAL WORKS, REferences to architecture are almost as rare in Indian as in any other old literature. There are, however, enough of such allusions, and so poetical, as to show very clearly that Indian architecture was no accident, but did very really correspond to an enthusiasm such as we can hardly conceive in connection with our modern cities.

Lankā, in the *Rāmāyana*, is likened to a mind-wrought city in the air ; and again, to a beautiful woman, with banners for her earrings and the towers upon the walls for her breasts. And this image we meet with once more a millennium and a half later, in the *Mahāvamsa*, when the chronicle tells us that a king of Kandy "raised for himself a monument of glory by building a wall enclosing the great *bō*-tree, the *chaitya*, and the Nātha *devāle* that stood in the middle of the city—a wall of stone, thick, high, and shining with plaster work, like unto a beautiful string of pearls adorning the neck of the city that was like a fair woman."

The Indians indeed loved their cities, "abounding in white houses." Bāna (7th century A.D.) compares Ujjayinī to Kailāsa, with its many peaks clear-cut against the sky, "for joy at being Shiva's home." The light-hearted folk that dwell there "order the making of water-works, bridges, temples, pleasure-grounds, wells, hostels, cattle-sheds, and halls of assembly"; they are masters of the whole circle of the arts; and the city is like the magic tree that grants all wishes: "its courts are open to all, yet its glory is undimmed." On the other hand, the ruin of Polonnāruva is described (13th century A.D.) in the *Mahāvamsa*, with an even more significant sadness; "its palaces and temples are tumbling down, because there is nothing to support them. Sad, indeed, is it also to see others, unable to stand by reason of decay and weakness, bending down to their fall day by day, like unto old men."

Town planning was no secular matter, but according to sacred traditions recorded in the *Shilpashāstras*. The proper place for each kind of building was strictly prescribed, as well as the measurements of the actual buildings down to the smallest mouldings. The whole was modelled upon the plan of a city in heaven; when the king desired to build, he called his architect, saying, "Send to the city of the gods, and procure me a plan of their palace, and build one like it." Thus all human building is traced back to the work of the divine architect, Vishvakarmā; and architecture, like painting and sculpture, becomes a hieratic and sacred calling, with the master-craftsman as priest. These conceptions belong not only to the past, but survive to the present day in the traditions of the builders' guilds.

The beginnings of Indian architecture have left no traces, for almost the first use of permanent material is in the 3rd century B.C., and the remains of that date already belong to a perfected style. When a little later we meet with the excavated *chaitya*-halls, and, later still, the earliest Hindū temples of the Āryā-varta and the Dravidian school, we are again faced with the same problem, of the origin of styles which seem to spring into being fully developed.

It is clear that architecture had not made much progress amongst the Āryans when they first entered India; on the contrary, all the later styles have been clearly shown to be developments of aboriginal and non-Āryan structures built of wood (posts and beams, bamboo, thatch), the intermediate stages being worked out in brick. The primitive wooden and brick building survives to the present day side by side with the work in stone, a silent witness of historic origins.

Some of the details of the early stone architecture point to Assyrian origins, but this connection is, for India, prehistoric. How the use of stone was first suggested is a matter of doubt; none of the early forms have a Greek character, but (like the Sānchī gates) are translations of Indian wooden forms into stone; while stone did not come into use for the structural temples of the Brāhmans until so late as the 6th century A.D.

The earliest form of architecture of which we have abundant remains is that of the more or less dome-shaped monuments (*chaityas*) (figs. 23, 79), constructed of solid brick or stone (except for the hollow relic chamber), and called *stūpas* ("topes") in India, and *dāgabas* in Ceylon. These monuments are usually Buddhist, occasionally Jain, never Brāhmanical. The most ancient (Sānchī) are plain domes usually with a spire and surrounded by a "Buddhist railing" as a protection against evil spirits. These railings (fig. 79) are massive stone copies of wooden post and rail fences, the three rails probably symbolising the "triple refuge" (Buddha, Dharma, Sangha): slightly later (Bharhut, Amarāvatī), the railings are ornamented with elaborate decorative and narrative sculpture. The stūpas vary from miniature votive models, to the largest at Anurādhapura, exceeding in size all but the two greatest of the Egyptian pyramids. Stūpas are not temples, but monuments erected over sacred relics, or to mark a sacred place. Their origin is somewhat doubtful: they are probably older than Buddhism, and some regard them as derived from the primitive earthen sepulchral mound, while others have traced their form to that of a primitive circular wooden hut-shrine. The most important examples are at Sānchī and Bharhut (2nd century B.C.), Amarāvatī and Sārnāth (6th century A.D.), in India, and Anurādhapura (3rd century B.C. to 8th A.D.) and Polonnāruva in Ceylon. The Ceylon *Shilpashāstras* preserve canons of form and proportion for six different types, called by such names as Bell-shape, Heap of rice, Lotus, and Bubble.

It is important to remark that the globular stūpa dome-form was not confined to solid monuments or miniature votive dāgabas, but was also a common feature of the open structural shrines, as represented at Bharhut, Amarāvatī and Ajantā.

Somewhat later than the earliest stūpas and railings are the great stone gateways, or *toran*, of which the finest and most perfectly preserved examples are at Sānchī (fig. 79). These are clearly copied from wooden forms. Those at Sānchī are completely covered with delicate sculptures that present us with a most interesting and intimate series of pictures of contemporary Indian life, including many very instructive representations of civil and secular architecture. No such gateways are found in Ceylon: but some of the *dāgabas* have, on the other hand, elaborate altars or "reredos" on the four sides, flanked with carved monolithic pillars of moderate height, with ornamentation somewhat reminiscent of Amarāvatī.

Another most important class of early buildings, and one purely Buddhist, is that of the *chaitya*-halls (Buddhist temples). Of free-standing structural examples of this type there survive only two with the original barrel roof intact. The vast majority must have been built of wood, upon a brick foundation, and have now perished. The prototype perhaps survives in the dairy temple of the Todas. We are well acquainted with the structural peculiarities of the *chaitya*-halls, from the many examples excavated in solid rock. These have barrel roofs, like the inverted hull of a ship, with every detail of the woodwork accurately copied in stone. The earliest date from the time of Asoka (3rd century B.C.) and are characterised by their single-arched entrance and plain façade. In later examples (fig. 80) the single-arched opening is reduced in size and becomes a window repeated above a smaller doorway, while the whole façade is often covered with sculptured figures. The characteristic arched window survives as an almost universal ornament in later architecture, particularly in Southern India (figs. 83, 88, 118), and Ceylon. The wooden prototype of these pointed arched entrances and win-

ous, is the Iron Pillar of Delhi, a monument erected by Samudragupta about 415 A.D. There are many beautiful mediæval Jain and Hindū pillars; those of the Jains in the Kanara district are especially graceful and well-proportioned, while there is a beautiful Hindū example outside the great temple at Purī.

In Ceylon no separate monoliths have been discovered, but some of the early dāgabas (Thūpārāma, etc.) are surmounted by very graceful and tall stone pillars with carved capitals, in place of the more usual Buddhist railing. These pillars perhaps supported a light roof, and served for the attachment of festoons of lamps on all festive occasions.

Not only the single *lāts*, but also the supporting columns of excavated and structural temples, are of great interest, so much so that the latter might alone demand a separate monograph. There are four especially characteristic forms, the early Persepolitan type, with kneeling bulls or other animals, and three distinctively Indian types, one with foliage overfalling from a vase-shaped capital, another with a ribbed cushion capital (figs. 81, 82) resembling the *āmalaka* of the Āryāvarta *shikhara*, the third and simplest form square in section, with a simple bracket capital supporting the horizontal beams of the roof, whether wood or stone (figs. 89, 98). By chamfer-

are the priests' chambers, are of four stages. The stages have dragon projections and coloured eaves; the pearl-red pillars, carved and ornamented, the richly adorned balustrades, and the roofs covered with tiles that reflect the light in a thousand shades, these things add to the beauty of the scene." Of Nālandā only traces are now recognisable, and of the "Brazen Monastery" at Anurādhapura there remain only the 1600 monolithic pillars which originally supported a splendid wooden superstructure, "built after the model of a palace of the devas." There are also at Anurādhapura remains of many smaller *pansalas*, or monks' houses, with their characteristic flights of steps (fig. 85), wing-stones, and "moonstones," the latter being semicircular doorsteps carved with animal processions (horse, elephant, lion, bull, and *hamsa*, or sacred goose) and lotus centres.

We have still to refer to the early secular buildings. We know practically nothing of them from actual remains : but there are so many good pictures of them at Sānchī, Bharhut, etc., sculptured in low relief, that we can tell exactly what they were like. The ground floor was probably used for shops or for cattle; a second story was supported on pillars. A narrow verandah runs along the second story, protected by a "Buddhist railing," while the rooms be-

century Jaisamand lake at Udaipur is some nine miles long by five broad; but it was only notably in Ceylon that there existed conditions favourable to the construction of very large works at a much earlier date. The largest of the embankments of these Ceylon reservoirs measures nine miles in length, and the area of the greatest exceeds 6000 acres. The earliest large tank dates from the 4th century B.C. What is even more remarkable than the amount of labour devoted to these works, is the evidence they afford of early skill in engineering, particularly in the building of sluices: those of the 2nd or 3rd century B.C. forming the type of all later examples in Ceylon, and anticipating some of the most important developments of modern construction. The most striking features of these sluices are the valve pits (rectangular wells placed transversely across the culverts and lined with close-fitting masonry), and the fact that the sectional area of the culverts enlarges towards the outlet, proving that the engineers were aware that retardation of the water by friction increased the pressure, and might have destroyed the whole dam if more space were not provided. Such contrivances, of course, remain hidden under water; but we find, both in Ceylon and in India, that the smaller reservoirs and bathing pools (fig. 84) built

abundance of temples which seem to spring into being
without any trace of historic origins. The explana-
tion of this circumstance is again to be found in the
loss of earlier buildings constructed of perishable
materials; all the great architectural types must have
been worked out in timber and brick before the erection of the stone temples which alone remain. One
point of particular interest is the fact that the early
temples of the gods, and prototypes of later forms,
seem to have been cars, conceived as self-moving
and rational beings. In the *Rāmāyana* it is said that
in Ayodhyā there were so many shrines that it seemed as if it were the very home of the living cars of the
gods: and in another place, the whole city of Ayodhyā is compared to a celestial car. The carrying of images in processional cars is still an important feature
of Hindū ritual. The resemblance of the Āryāvarta
shikhara to the bamboo scaffolding of a processional
car is too striking to be accidental. More than that,
we actually find stone temples of great size provided
with enormous stone wheels (Konārak, Vijayanagar): and the monolithic temples at Māmallapuram
(7th century) (fig. 83) are actually called *rathas*, that
is cars, while the term *vimāna*, applied to later
Dravidian temples, has originally the same sense, of
vehicle or moving palace. Something of the sense

of life belonging to the older vehicles remains associated with the later buildings: it has been well said, that "in Indian temples, we feel an infinite power of increase."

The essential parts of a Hindū temple are the nave or porch, with or without pillars, and open to all twice-born men; and a square shrine containing the image and entered only by the officiating priests, but often with a passage for circumambulation, by worshippers. The nave has a flat or comparatively low roof, while the shrine is covered by a spire or *shikhara*. The whole temple with its subsidiary chapels and other buildings is usually surrounded by a high wall, with entrances on four sides.

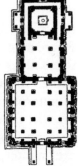

Plan of Pāpanātha temple at Pattakadal. After Fergusson. Scale 50 feet to 1 inch.

Hindū temples are built not for men, but for the god and his service. The idol may be no more than a plain *lingam*, but, once consecrated, it becomes a special mode of the god-consciousness, and for this reason no expenditure and no labour have seemed to his devout worshippers too great to be lavished on his sanctuary. Nowadays we conceive that churches should correspond in number to the local population, and are satisfied with any building, however mean, if it shelters a sufficient congregation. Such ideas were far from the mind of the Indian builders: their cathedral towns came into being for the churches, not the churches for the towns; while sometimes they built whole cities (*e.g.* Bhuvaneshwar, Palītāna, etc.) of temples for the gods alone, visited by none but priests and pilgrims. The Hindū shrine is essentially a place for pilgrimages and circumambulations, where men come for *darshan*, to "see" the god. In all these ideas the Indian and the mediæval European cathedral builders were essentially at one: not only in external forms, but in underlying spirit, Gothic art was a flowering of the Oriental consciousness in Europe. Gothic art and Roman Catholic Christianity are an interpretation of the East, while modern cities and the Protestant consciousness hold East and West for ever apart.

The two great styles of Hindū architecture are the Āryāvarta or Indo-Āryan, found throughout Hindustān from Gūjarāt to Bengal and Orissa: and the Dravidian, in Southern India and Ceylon. The style called Chalukyan, intermediate in character and distribution, belongs to the Deccan and Mysore.

The chief feature of the Āryāvarta style (fig. 86) is the bulging spire (*shikhara*) with carved ribs, rising above the shrine and constantly used on a smaller scale, often repeated upon itself, as an architectural ornament. The *shikhara* is capped by a huge ribbed stone (*āmalaka*) of flattened circular cushion form, with a stone vase above this. The earliest phase of the northern style, however, appears in the excavated caves, where the relation to the structural temples appears most evidently in the form of the carved pillars (fig. 82). The spire has analogies on the one hand with the wooden processional car, on the other with the Buddhist *stūpa*, the relic chamber of the latter corresponding to the *garbha* of the Hindū shrine. It may be mentioned here that Hindū and modern Buddhist temples have often been spoken of as "pagodas." In point of fact, the Chinese pagoda form is of Indian Buddhist derivation; the superposition of roofs which constitutes its chief peculiarity is a development of the old Buddhist motif of the *chatta*, or umbrella,—the symbol of regal honour which usually crowned the solid *stūpas* and structural domes. Hindū temples of the pagoda type are frequent in the Panjāb Himālayas, and Buddhist "pagodas" in Nepāl, Burma, and Ceylon; but the same multiplication of roofs is also recognisable in other areas (*cf.* fig. 86).

The oldest structural example in the northern style

is a brick temple at Bhitargaon, perhaps of the 4th century; and from the 7th century onwards there is an abundance of stone temples. Amongst the oldest are the 7th-century Vaishnava temple at Aihole, the 7th–8th century Parashurāmeshwar and Muktesh-war temples at Bhuvaneshwar, and Jain temples at Aihole and elsewhere in the Dharwar district, and the 8th-century Hindū temples at Osia in the Jodhpur state. The fine examples at Khajurāho (*ca.* 1000 A.D.), Bhuvaneshwar (10th century), and Purī (12th century) illustrate a second phase where the *shikhara* has become much higher and proportionately more slen-der. The Great Temple at Bhuvaneshwar, with its many smaller buildings clustered about the huge spire, is one of the most impressive of all Hindū shrines. Later than the Great Temple are the Raj-rāni Temple at Bhuvaneshwar, decorated with col-umns and statues set in niches, as if on the façade of a Gothic cathedral: and the 13th century ruined temple of the Sun at Konārak, perhaps more splen-didly designed and lavishly decorated than any other in India.

The mediæval western Jain style of Kāthiāwār and Gūjarāt is distinguished by its use of very richly car-ved columns, strut brackets, and elaborately carved domed ceilings with central pendants. Some of these features appear also in the fine woodwork of secular buildings of towns such as Surāt, Ahmadābād, and even Bombay. The most splendid temples are those of Mt. Ābū (1031 and 1230 A.D.); somewhat similar must have been the famous temple of Somnāth (Shiva) destroyed by Mahmūd about 1000 A.D. Most remarkable, also, are the Jain temple cities (11th century or older, present day) at Palītāna and Girnar, the former containing over 500 shrines without any secular building whatever. There are two beautiful Jain towers, respectively of the 10th and 15th century, at Chitōr.

The mediæval Āryāvarta style gradually passes into a modern phase, characterised by a slenderer and almost straight-sided tower, constantly repeated on itself as an architectural ornament; the modern temples of Benāres, Delhi, Ahmadābād, and most other parts of Hindustān, are of this type. A Bengālī variety has a roof with curved outline, and overhanging eaves derived, like the Rājput *jhārokha*, from bent bamboo and thatched prototypes.

The Dravidian temples are clearly distinguished from those of Hindustān by their great towers horizontally divided in terraces, and by the form of the roof, either a barrel roof (fig. 83) of the old *chaitya*-hall type, or a globular dome. These roof types are taken over directly from the old Buddhist forms.

Buddhist, Dravidian, and Rājput domes.

The dome is usually ribbed, affording clear vestigial evidence of an original construction dependent on the elasticity of bent bamboo; thus the Dravidian and Āryāvarta *shikharas* are actually closely related; the one has developed in height and is differently terminated, the other retains a bulbous form. The Āryāvarta dome has never been adapted to secular purposes; but the Dravidian dome, always recognisable by the lotus moulding or calyx beneath and inverted lotus (*mahā-padma*) above the actual globe, reappears in the Rājput *chhatrīs*, and is, moreover, the predominating element in the design of even such typical Indo-Muhammadan domes as those of the Tāj, or the Bījāpur tombs. The globular motif is also constantly recognisable in metal work (*e.g.* figs. 115, 117, 122).

lier is the beautiful Mālegitti Shivālaya at Bādāmī, which is very like the Māmallapuram *rathas*, and has also a small porch with four massive pillars recalling the type of the Ajantā caves, Nos. 1 and 17.

The earliest of the structural temples in the south are the sea-shore temple at Māmallapuram, and the great temples at Tanjore and Gangaikondapuram, and the smaller Subrahmaniya temple at Tanjore. These, except the last, are the work of Chola kings of a little before and after 1000 A.D. The Subrahmaniya temple is finely proportioned, and covered with a profusion of delicate ornament (fig. 88). An interesting tradition relates that the king himself came to see the master sculptor at work, and stood behind him as he was intent upon his carving; then the sculptor held out his hand without turning, to receive a fresh wad of betel from his servant and pupil, and the king, unseen, placed a royal betel leaf in the sculptor's hand. He, when he began to chew it, recognised the unusual delicacy of the condiments, and turned in fear to ask the king's pardon; but the king answered, " I am a king of men: but you are a king of craftsmen, and merit royal delicacies."

Before the middle of the 14th century the second phase (1350–1750 A.D.) of the Dravidian style had been elaborated—probably in wooden forms, and

ARCHITECTURE

for some features perhaps also in terra-cotta. The most characteristic feature of this style is found in its pillared halls, whether open naves (*mantapams*, as at Vellore) or separate "choultries." These halls are roofed with horizontal stone slabs, and have most elegant cornices with a double flexure, supported on delicate pseudo-wooden transoms: the pillars, though monolithic, are often of compound design, and may be combined with figures of monsters (*yālis*), rearing horses, gods or *shaktis*, warriors, dancing-girls, or other motifs. The style culminates at Vijayanagar and Tādpatri in the 16th century; and in the even more exquisite Avadaiyār Kōvil, probably of the same date (fig. 90); the last exhibits very well the wonderful refinement, vitality, and mystery of this best phase of the later Dravidian style.

The last and most productive form of the Dravidian style is distinguished by its enormous towering gateways, extensive corridors, and multiplicity of buildings included within the high encircling walls. The high external walls and gateways (*gopurams*) often completely dwarf the original shrine. The best-known example is the great temple at Madurā (fig. 89) built for Tirumalai Nāyyak during the years 1623 to 1625, and the elaborate three-aisled "choultry" (*chattram*) in front of it. The great corridors, about 4000 feet in all, at Rāmeshwaram are almost equally remarkable.

The more conspicuous secular forms of Dravidian architecture, the 17th and 18th century palaces at Madurā and Tanjore, are of little interest. Quite the reverse, however, is true of the domestic wooden building; much of this, dating from the 18th century, preserves far older traditions, and is wonderfully beautiful. The ordinary thatched, one-storied house, of the South Indian and Ceylon type, consists of rooms grouped about a square open court, and separated from it by a wide covered verandah where all household work is carried on; there may be a second verandah, long and narrow, facing the street. The wooden forms of interest are the inner and outer verandah pillars, ceilings, cornices, and doorways, and these often serve to throw much light on the history of the ecclesiastical buildings in stone (figs. 95 to 98).

The chief characteristics of the Chalukyan or Hoysala style of the Deccan and Mysore are the high and very richly carved plinth, the star-shaped ground plan, and low pyramidal roof. The best-known examples are at Belūr (*ca.* 1117 A.D.) and Halebīd (12th to 13th century). Temples in the Bellary district, though built by Chalukyan kings and most ornate, are more Dravidian than Chalukyan in design.

ARCHITECTURE

One other and quite isolated style of temple building to which reference must be made, is that of Kāshmīr (8th to 13th century). This is a style with pointed arches, and is partly derived from Western classic models; the most important example is the temple
of the sun at Mārtand, built by Lalitāditya in the
8th century. No traces of this ancient style survive
in later Kāshmīr art, which is for the most part of
Indian origin in the 14th century, and in its recent
forms distinctly of Musulmān character. Kāshmīr
thus affords a strong contrast with Nepāl, another
great Himālayan state which has preserved old
Buddhist traditions of architecture and sculpture up
to the present day.

We have so far left out of account the splendid
civil architecture of Hindustān. This is best exemplified in the palaces and cenotaphs of the Rājput
chiefs (Jodhpur, Bikaner, Udaipur, Gwaliar, etc.), the
houses of wealthy merchants (Bikaner, Jaisalmer,
etc.), and the riverside *ghāts* (Benāres, Ujjain, Har-
dwar, etc.). There are no prouder nor more splendid
buildings in the world than the Rājput palaces, nor
built on finer sites. We often think nowadays of building as a desecration of natural beauty, because it has
in Europe for so long actually been so; but these
palaces, crowning the summits of lofty crags or flat-

topped hills, fortified on every side, or overlooking lakes or reservoirs, seem to be a living part of the soil on which they stand, and themselves have somewhat of the grandeur and nobility of mountains. The most conspicuous features of detail in the Rājput palaces and contemporary domestic architecture are the curved overhanging cornices (*jhārokha*) (fig. 94), the small domes, plain or ribbed, and the massive bastions of the larger buildings. The *jhārokha* form recalls the curved roof and overhanging eaves of one of the *rathas* at Māmallapuram, and both derive from the curved overhanging thatched roof of primitive domestic buildings.

Scarcely any palaces now standing are older than the 13th century. Most of those at Chitōr are later than Alāu-d-din's raid in 1303; the 15th-century palace of Kumbha Rāna is especially beautiful. The finest of the old Rājput palaces, however, is that of Mān Singh (1486–1518) at Gwaliar (fig. 91), with additions by his successor and subsequently by Jahāngīr and Shāh Jahān. The Mughal emperor Bābur saw it in 1527, and has recorded his admiration as follows: "They are singularly beautiful palaces . . . wholly of hewn stone . . . the small domes are one on each side of the greater, according to the custom of Hindustān. The five large domes are covered with plates of copper gilt. The outside of the walls they have inlaid with green painted tiles. All around they have inlaid the walls with figures of plantain trees made of painted tiles."

Next in importance to Gwaliar is the palace at Amber near the quite modern city of Jaipur; but it is a century later, and is less purely Hindū. This palace is mainly the work of another Mān Singh, the friend of Akbar; to whom also is due a fine *ghāt* and observatory on the riverside at Benāres.

Less imposing than Gwaliar, and more exquisite than even Amber, is the late 16th-century palace at Udaipur, where the Sesodia dynasty founded a new capital after the fall of Chitōr. Additions to the original building, in perfect accord with the design, have been made from time to time up to the present day. The famous *tripulia* (three-arched gate) leads to a terrace which extends the whole length of the palace. This terrace is built up fifty feet from the ground on triple arches, over the slope of the hill away from the palace; and though it is thus hollow beneath, it has a range of stables built along the outer edge, and can support the Mahārāja's whole army, elephants, cavalry, and infantry, when assembled for review. On the lake are two small islands, with palaces and pavilions of the 17th and 18th centuries : Fergusson thought these island palaces the most beautiful things of their kind in the world.

More masculine in character is the palace at Jodhpur (fig. 92), built up on a high crag overlooking the city; the whole rock is faced with masonry and fortified with bastions or half-round towers of great solidity, on the summit of which rests the airy superstructure of the palace itself. There are other splendid palaces at Bikaner, Dīg, Datiya, Ūrchā, and some twenty more of the Rājput capitals. Jaipur is interesting as a well-planned and on the whole well-built modern city.

The Rājputs have also erected many beautiful cenotaphs, usually in the form of a *chhatrī* raised on the spot where the body was burnt. Such monuments are grouped together in some wooded or secluded spot a little distance from the town: they commemorate not only the departed warrior prince, but also the widow or widows who would not be separated from him even by death. Fergusson watched the erection of one of these monuments in 1839. "From its architect," he says, " I learned more of the secrets of art as practised in the Middle Ages than I have learned from all the books I have since read."

The best examples of 19th-century architecture

are the *utris* or residences and hostels of the Rājput princes, built along the *ghāts* at Benāres. The
Ghonslā Ghāt of the princes of Nāgpur is illustrated
in fig. 93. It is a style such as this, and such as that
of the palaces of Rājputāna, which is still a living
tradition in Hindustān, and could be utilised
in the making of the new Delhi.

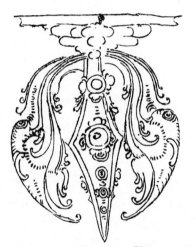

Engraved design from a copper-plate grant: Silahara, 11th century A.D.

103. Gargoyle. Brass. 17-18 c. Nepāl. Prof. Tagore's collection, Calcutta.
104. Lamps. Brass. 17-19 c. Nepāl. Sir E. L. Durand Collection.
105. Vessel with lid. *Bidrī*. 4½ in. Bidar. Author.
106. Fish. *Bidrī*. Orissa. Mr. Justice Holmwood.
107. Horse. *Bidrī*. 18-19 c. Rājputana. Prof. Tagore.

108. Betel tray. Gold and gems. Diam. 13⅝ in. 18 c. Sinhalese.
Temple of the Tooth. Kandy, Ceylon.

109. *Huka* cover. Silver on copper. 3¼ in. diam. 17-18 c. Purniah,
Bengal.

110. Lime box with chain and spoon. Gold, very finely chased,
2⅓ in. diam. Kandy, Ceylon.

111. Lamp. Brass. 16 c. (?) Orissa. E. R. Lindsay.

112. Water-vessel. Brass. 19 c. Tanjore.

113. Milk pot. Bronze. 2½ in. 19 c. Oude or Bihār.
114. Lime box. Silver on copper. 18 c. Sinhalese, Colombo Museum, Colombo.
115. Water vessel (*surāhi*). Brass. 18-19 c. 9¾ in. Bihār or Bengal.
116. Tray-stand. Bronze. 16 c. 9½ in. Nepāl or Bengal. Museum of Fine Arts, Boston.
117. Milk jug. Silver. 18-19 c. 6 in. Amritsar. Author.
118. Comb. Brass. 17 c. So. India. F. O. Oertel.
119. Comb (handle composed of four deer with two heads). Brass. 8⅝ in. 17 c. (?) Victoria and Albert Museum, Crown Copyright.

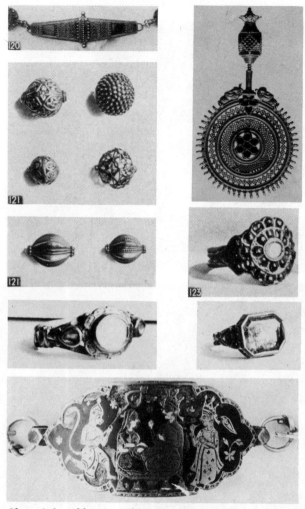

120. Clasp (of necklace). Gold. 2¾ in. 18 c. Jaffna, Ceylon. Author.
121. Six beads (filigree and repoussé). Gold. 18 c. ⅝ in. Jaffna, Ceylon. Author.
122. Earring. Gold. 18 c. 2⅛ in. So. India. Museum of Fine Arts, Boston.
123. Finger-ring (gold embedding, flat diamond and rubies). So. Indian. Author.
124. Finger-ring. Gold enamel, flat diamond. Jaipur.
125. Finger-ring. Gold enamel and emerald. Jaipur.
126. Enamelled armlet (Rāma, Sitā, Lakshman and Hanuman). Gold and enamel. Formerly Goloubew Collection.

127. Filigree waist-chain. Silver. 18 c. Kandy. Colombo Museum.
128. Rosary bead (*rudrāksha mālā*, "Gauri-shankar"). Gold. 19 c.
Belonged to a Shaiva priest, Colombo.
129. Pendant (*kuralla-padak-kama*). Gold, gems and pearls. 5½
x 2¾ in. 18 c. Kandy. Halangoda, Kandy.
130. Knife. Silver-mounted (pierced and repoussé). 3 in. 18 c.
Kandy. A. R. Casse Lebbe.
131. Areca-nut slicer. Brass, silver damascened, steel blade. 8 in.
18 c. Kandy. Formerly the author's collection.

132. Krishna, by Gobind Ratan. Abt. 1830. Ivory. Nayagarh, Orissa.
133. Compasses. Ivory. 17 c. 6¼ in. Kandy. Colombo Museum.
134. Door-guardian (*dwāra-pāla*). Ivory. 16-17 c. 11¹⁄₁₆ x 3⅝ in. Kandy. Formerly the author's collection.
135. Door lintel. Ivory and ebony. Ridī Vihāra, Ceylon.

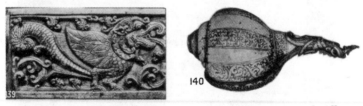

136. Ivory casket. Before 18 c. Travancore. Victoria and Albert Museum, Crown Copyright.
137. Detail of a two-wheeled carriage. Ivory veneer, engraved and inlaid with colored lac. 17-18 c. Palace, Tanjore.
138. Detail of a two-wheeled carriage. Ivory plaque centre. 17 c. Palace, Tanjore.
139. Panel. Ivory. Kandy. Victoria and Albert Museum, Crown Copyright.
140. Conch. Chank trumpet "Shankha." Engraved and inlaid with lac, brass mounting, with gold and silver inlay. 18 c. Udanuwara, Ceylon.

CHAPTER FIFTH   METAL WORK, ENAMELS, AND JEWELLERY

THE INDIAN KNOWLEDGE OF METALlurgy is both wide and ancient. The famous Iron Pillar of Chandragupta II. at Delhi shows that already in the 5th century A.D. the Indians were able to forge masses of iron larger than any which European foundries could deal with before the latter part of the 19th century. It is remarkable that this pillar, though fully exposed to the weather, has never rusted, but retains its inscription as clear as when it was engraved. There is a still larger iron column at Dhār, over 42 feet in length (about 321 A.D.). The great iron beams of the 13th century at Konārak are less remarkable, as they are made up of many small bars imperfectly welded. Another important example is the 24-feet wrought-iron gun at Nurvar. Not only was iron worked at an early date (being mentioned with gold, silver, lead, and tin in the *Yajurveda*), but there existed (and perhaps originated) in India a very early knowledge of the art of preparing steel; the steel of India was known to the Greeks and Persians, and very probably to the Egyptians, and was also the material of the famous blades of Damascus. The manufacture on a small scale has survived to the present day in India and Ceylon; clay crucibles containing about 12 oz. of iron, and chips

137

of wood, are heated in a blast furnace until the contents are melted, forming ultimately the little bars of hard steel which are handed over to the blacksmith to be worked up into tools and weapons. The subject of Indian arms and armour is so vast, that it would be impossible to give any detailed account of it here; but mention must be made of the more important forms of decoration. Best of all is the art of carving steel, which attained such perfection in Tanjore and other parts of Southern India, where it no longer flourishes, and in Rājputāna, where the armourers still work. Superb examples from Tanjore are in the Madras Museum: the elephant goad of fig. 99 belongs to the Rāja of Ettayapuram in the far south; while there are fine collections of chiselled and damascened arms in all the Rājput palaces.

There are many types of damascening (*koft*) and encrusting—the inlay or overlay of one metal on another,—all of them practised throughout India, or at least in several widely separated localities, and often combined in one and the same piece of work. In the simplest and cheapest method, the steel or iron basis is first roughened by scoring with fine scratches, then gold or silver wire is pressed down according to the required design, and well hammered. Good work of this kind is still done at Sialkot in the

METAL WORK

Panjāband in Travancore. From this there are transitions to the proper inlaying of wire in deep grooves
cut in the ground metal: when hammered down, the
wire is tightly held by the sides of the grooves, and
the surface may be filed and polished. Gold or silver
on steel, and silver or brass on copper, are the usual
combinations. In another sort of work, frequently
combined with the wire inlay, small plates of the
encrusting metal are inlaid on excavated areas of
the ground, the edges of which areas are hammered
over to grip the inlaid plate.

A familiar example of quite flat incrustation, usually combined with wire inlay (as in the rich example,
fig. 105, also fig. 187) is seen in the well-known *bidrī*
ware. This is an alloy of zinc, lead, and tin, from
which are made dishes, basins, pandans, etc., used
both by Hindūs and Musulmāns. It is, however, an
old Hindū art, taking its name from Bidār in the
Deccan. Another important centre was Purnea in
Bengal, where also flourished a special local style
of silver inlay on copper, combined with inset silver *ajourée* (fig. 109). After the silver inlay is completed, the surface of the *bidrī* ware is chemically
blackened.

In some types of encrusted ware the excavated
area is carved or repoussé, forming a raised design

to which the thin overlay readily adapts itself when hammered down. Much of the most florid work of this sort is of modern manufacture in Tanjore, and a reflection of the same technique appears in a form of Lucknow *bidrī*, where the silver overlay is raised in relief. But the flat incrustation is almost always more pleasing and richer in effect without a suggestion of overloading.

In old work also, copper only is overlaid on the brass; the modern use of silver has a somewhat tawdry effect.

Of great importance, both from a practical point of view and from an æsthetic, are the vessels entirely of brass or copper, used by Hindūs for ritual and domestic purposes. Brass does not appear to have been in use before the 11th century; before that time all vessels were made of bronze or copper, as many still are.

An extract from the *Mahānirvāna Tantra* will show with what pious and devoted affection objects intended for ritual use were manufactured:

" The jar is called *kalasha*, because Vishvakarmā made it from the different parts of each of the Devatās. It should be thirty-six fingers in breadth in its widest part and sixteen in height. The neck should be four fingers in breadth, the mouth six, and the base five. This is the rule for the design of the *kalasha*.

METAL WORK

"It should be made . . . without hole or crack. In its making all miserliness should be avoided, since it is fashioned for the pleasure of the Devas."

Temple lamps (figs. 102, 104, 111) are of infinite variety: the most characteristic are the standing lamps in the form of a branching tree, each branch ending in a little bowl for oil and wick. Others are simple upright stands, supporting a shallow bowl arranged for several wicks; and very frequently the central rod ends in a bird finial, usually a *hamsa* or a peacock. Similar lamps are also suspended by chains, which are themselves richly varied in design and excellent in workmanship. Lamps in the Buddhist temples of Ceylon are often hollow, containing oil which continually refills the small mouth containing the wick; some of these also are in bird form. Perhaps the greatest variety of all kinds of standing and other lamps is found in Nepāl (fig. 104). Another frequent form is that of a standing woman, holding forth a shallow bowl for oil and wick (fig. 111). A beautiful form of lamp for burning camphor before an image consists of a little bowl, enclosed in the centre of a many-petaled lotus, made to open and close. The same lotus form enshrines the Buddhist goddess Vajra-Tārā, who is seated in the centre, while eight reflexes of herself (for each point of the

compass) are represented on the eight petals (fig. 101).
There are many good forms of ceremonial spoons;
some also for serving rice, but none, of course, for
eating, for which all Hindūs and Musulmāns use
their fingers.

Incised decoration of a Tanjore *lotā*.

Domestic brass is the glory of a Hindū kitchen;
it is cleaned daily, and polished to a degree that must
be seen to be believed. Most important are the large
and small *lotās* for water, and smaller vessels with a
wide mouth for milk (fig. 113); then all sorts of shal-
lower bowls and dishes for cooking rice, some of
which, belonging to communities or guilds, are of
enormous size—cauldrons rather than bowls; then
other vessels for special purposes, of which perhaps
the finest are the *surāhis* (fig. 115), globular in shape
with a long narrow neck, used for Ganges water, and
carried all over India.

The use of gold plate is naturally restricted to the

METAL WORK

most wealthy, but silver dishes are in common use
for table service of the well-to-do. A silver jug for
feeding a child with milk is shown in fig. 117; this
form, with or without a lid, occurs all over India, in
silver, copper, and brass, and is that used from early
times onward for the ceremonial ratification of gifts
by pouring water, also for drinking purposes, the
water being poured from the spout to the mouth
without contact. It will be seen, from the thorough
daily cleansing to which all domestic vessels are sub-
jected, scouring, in fact, with mud, that no sort of
raised ornament is appropriate; hence the only decoration applied to such vessels, whether originally
cast or hammered, takes the form of incised design,
or quite flat encrustation.

Incised decoration of a Tanjore *lotā*.

Long-toothed metal combs are used for hair-dress-
ing, but flowers and jewels only for its adornment.
Of two combs illustrated here, one (fig. 118) shows

the use of architectural ornament of the Dravidian cornice and *chaitya*-window type ; the second (fig. 119), a 16th-century piece from Tanjore, is surmounted by four deer, the heads and bodies so arranged that the three prongs do duty for eight horns, and eight legs for the sixteen which four quadrupeds should possess.

Repoussé or engraved trays in silver or brass are used for all kinds of offerings, and for conveying gifts, but especially for flowers to be offered in temples. The old Sīgiri paintings represent a procession of court ladies (or perhaps *apsarās*) attended by maids bearing trays of flowers.

Nowhere has a local style and good workmanship in brass and bell-metal been better maintained up to recent times than in Nepāl. Even images of some merit are still cast. Fig. 103 shows a characteristic gargoyle from a Nepalese temple; fig. 104 a group of lamps; and fig. 116 a tray stand, of which the main motif is a boldly drawn bull. The latter object may possibly be of Bengālī origin, the older traditions of Nepalese and Bengal art being very closely related. The *vajra* (Tib. *dorje*), or thunderbolt, is a common cult-object, often of fine design and workmanship. The copper and brass boxes are of very richly repoussé and pierced work. Beside the cast figures, there are many others beaten up in extraordinarily high relief.

The metal work of the Sinhalese is of special excellence and variety, speaking, that is, of the Kandyan provinces, rather than the low-country, where Portuguese and Dutch influences have long predominated. The nut-slicers (fig. 131) and lime-boxes (figs. 110, 114) are of inlaid copper or brass, sometimes repoussé or set with gems. In the larger temples there are still some beautiful vessels of gold and silver (fig. 108). Knife-sheaths and powder-horns are set in silver filigree ; knives are richly ornamented (fig. 130) ; the *devāle* shell trumpets (fig. 140) are elaborately mounted in brass, with inlay of silver and copper. The goldsmiths and painters are mostly of Indian extraction, but their works have several peculiar forms, such as the " coconut-flower " and " pepper-spike " chains. The damascened iron fittings of the temple doors are very noteworthy; everywhere the Kandyan *vihāras* bear witness to the lavish patronage of the great 18th-century king, Kīrti Shrī Rāja Simha, who, although a Hindū amongst Buddhists, " made himself one with the religion and the people," like another Akbar.

Almost the only Hindū coins of serious artistic merit are those of the earlier Guptas; the later Musulmān coins, with their fine decorative inscriptions, are admirable in quite a different way.

Many kinds of brass toys (figs. 106, 107) are to be bought in almost any bazar. The best are perhaps those from Rājputāna, where horses on wheels and horses or elephants drawing country carts with domed canopies, are favourite motifs. These carts must be just like the little clay cart (which ought to have been of gold) that gives its name to King Shudraka's drama, and the golden carts of the children mentioned in the *Pattinappālai*. More deliberately grotesque are the brass figures of horses and riders which used to be made at Vizagapatam. There is a considerable modern trade in Ceylon in realistic brass animals. Many of the old brass toys, as well as other objects such as lamps, and many types of heavy primitive jewellery in base metal, are decorated with twisted and spiral motifs, originally applied in the form of strings of rolled wax to the surface of the wax model before casting.

The same method of wax-casting is exemplified in the old Rājput (Bundi) craft of casting flexible chain anklets (*sānt*) in one piece. Sir Thomas Wardle, speaking of these in a lecture (1901), remarked: " I bought for a few annas a bronze chain anklet, but all cast in one mould together, quite a common thing,

146

but so wonderfully made that one of our best foundry
owners told me he did not think anyone could do it
in Europe." A composition of wax, resin, and oil is
prepared in a long string, and twisted spirally round
a stick of the diameter of the proposed links. One cut
along the stick separates the links: these are interlac-
ed every one into two others, and each one joined up
by applying a hot knife edge. When sixty or seventy
rings are thus united, the ends of the chain are joined
and the whole gently flattened and manipulated until it forms a perfectly flexible model of the future
anklet. It is then dipped several times into a paste
of clay and cow-dung until it is completely covered,
and then enclosed in a thicker coat of clay. When
dry, the upper edge of the mould is scraped so as to
expose the top of each link, and a wax leading line
attached, and again covered with clay. Two such
moulds are enclosed side by side in a stronger case
of clay and black earth, and the wax ends of the leading line are brought up into a cup-shaped hollow at
the top of the mould. This is filled with metal and a
little borax, and luted over and covered with clay
and earth, leaving only a small blow-hole. When this
mould is placed in a furnace and fired, the wax melts
and the metal takes its place; and after cooling the
mould is broken and the leading lines removed and

irregularities filed away, leaving a flexible metal anklet ready for use.

This is the ancient *cire-perdue* process, most skilfully and adroitly practised by quite illiterate craftsmen all over India. The technique of founding bronze, copper, and brass images is exactly similar, and here also work is still done of great delicacy and complexity. It may be remarked that the vast majority of fine metal images are of copper: bronze is rarely used, and, by the illustrations given here, only figs. 3 and 28 represent bronze originals. There is probably no branch of Indian metal work in which there is not still available a store of workshop skill and valuable recipes, from which the most experienced modern craftsmen and founders might profitably learn. The methods of manufacturing steel and iron afford another case in point, particularly in respect of the resistance to corrosion.

A thorough investigation of the many alloys known to Indian metallurgists is also very desirable. Beside such special alloys as *bidrī* and *pas-lō*, there is a great variety in colour and power of tarnish resistance in the various brasses and bell-metals. Indian brass is always superior in colour to the commercial sheet brass now in general use. The tawdry yellow of modern Benāres brass, by which Indian metal work

148

is best known to tourists and collectors, well match-
es its cheap and perfunctory workmanship; but old
brass is often scarcely less beautiful than gold.

From the earliest times the Indians have loved to
adorn themselves with jewels; indeed, the modern
work descends in an unbroken line from the primitive
and still surviving use of garlands of fresh flowers,
and of seeds; from these are derived the names of
the work in gold, such as *champa*-bud-necklace.
Many of the names of jewels mentioned in Pānini's
grammar (4th century B.C.) are still in use. The long
Panjābī necklaces are called "garlands of enchant-
ment," *mohan-māla*: earrings are called ear-flowers
(*karn-phūl*). The forms are suggestive, but never
imitative of the flower prototypes. Perhaps no people
in the world have loved jewellery so well as the Indians. It is a religious duty to provide a wife with jewels, as with dress; she should never appear before her
husband without them, but in his absence on a journey she should discard them temporarily, and after
his death, for ever.

One need be an Indian woman, born and bred in
the great tradition, to realise the sense of power
that such jewels as earrings and anklets lend their
wearers; she knows the full delight of swinging
jewels touching her cheek at every step, and the fas-

cination of the tinkling bells upon her anklets. Some have called her nose-rings barbarous and her love of jewels childish; but there are also those who think that she knows best what best becomes her.

All well-to-do families have their own goldsmith, whose office is hereditary : and since the goldsmiths are proverbially untrustworthy, it is usual for them to bring their tools and do whatever work is required at the patron's own house, under an overseer's eye. The dishonest goldsmith is described by Manu as the most hurtful of thorns, meriting to be cut to pieces with razors.

How splendid the old Indian jewellery (several centuries B.C.) could be is well suggested in a passage of the *Dhammapada*, describing the "great-creeper-parure," made by 500 goldsmiths in four months, and worn by the daughter of a king's treasurer : "When this parure was on, it extended from head to foot . . a part of this parure consisted of a peacock, and there were 500 feathers of red gold on the right side, and 500 on the left side. The beak was of coral, the eyes were of jewels, and likewise the neck and the tail feathers. The midribs of the feathers were of silver, and likewise the shanks of the legs. . . This parure was worth ninety millions,* and a hundred thousand

* Copper coins, weighing 146 grains.

was spent on the workmanship." It is not only, however, the daughters of treasurers who wear many
jewels; the peasant jewellery is of equal interest and
variety. In Southern India even the poorest coolies
wear gold ornaments.

The superfluity of wealth in an old Tamil seaport
at the mouth of the Kāverī is thus suggested in the
Pattinappālai, a poem of the earlier centuries of the
present Christian era : " The heavy earrings thrown
by the ladies of shining brows, shy glance and fair-
wrought jewels, at the fowls that peck the drying
grain in the spacious courts of the mighty city (are
so large and numerous as to) obstruct the passage
of the three-wheeled toy-carts, drawn without horses
by children whose anklets are of gold."

Paes gives the following description of the maids
of honour of the Vijayanagar queens early in the 16th
century: "They have very rich and fine silk cloths;
on the head they wear high caps (*cf.* fig. 51) ... and
on these caps they wear flowers made of large pearls;
collars on the neck with jewels of gold very richly
set with many emeralds and diamonds and rubies
and pearls ; and beside this many strings of pearls,
and others for shoulder-belts; on the lower part of
the arm many bracelets, with half of the upper arm
all bare, having armlets in the same way all of pre-

cious stones; on the waist many girdles of gold and of precious stones, which girdles hang in order one below the other, almost as far down as half the thigh; besides these belts they have other jewels, for they wear very rich anklets, even of greater value than the rest . . . in all perhaps sixty women fair and young, from sixteen to twenty years of age. Who is he that could tell of the costliness and the value of what each of these women carries on her person?"

Davy thus describes the costume of the last king of Kandy: "On state occasions, he was either dressed in the most magnificent robes, loaded with a profusion of jewellery, or in complete armour of gold, ornamented with rubies, emeralds, and diamonds."

In all Indian sculpture and painting, the jewellery, which often forms the greater part of the costume, and sometimes the whole of it, is represented with great fidelity; so that the materials exist for a most detailed history. But not only was jewellery worn by the gods, and by men, women, and children; classic Indian poetry makes constant reference to a similar decoration of palaces and cities, to say nothing of the jewelled trappings of elephants and horses and cattle, and the decoration of state carriages and beds. Architectural columns were hung with festoons of pearls, and these are invariably indicated in the old paintings and represented in the actual stone and woodwork. The classic drama of the *Little Clay Cart*, for example, speaks of "golden stairways inlaid with all sorts of gems," and of "crystal windows from which are hanging strings of pearls": "the arches set with sapphires look as though they were the home of the rainbow." It is in a court such as this that the jewellers are at work, setting rubies, fashioning golden ornaments, grinding coral, and piercing shell. "Upon its forehead," says Bāna, describing a coal-black steed, "dangled rings of fine gold, and . . . it was adorned with trappings of gold." Paes (*ca.* 1520) describes a room in the palace at Vijayanagar completely lined ("I do not say 'gilded,' but 'lined' inside") with gold, containing a bed "with a railing of pearls a span wide." A *shāstra* on ship-building mentions the garlands of pearls and gold hung from the carved prows.

There are also certain frequent forms of decorating the body by means of painting or tattooing; for example, the fingers and the soles of the feet of women are stained a clear red with henna (*hīnā*); tattooing is a common practice; and sectarian marks are applied by both men and women, chiefly to the forehead, by which their form of faith can be learnt

153

at a glance. In the same way, after the example of Shiva, his devotees are smeared with ashes, which they use as do the worldly their paste of fragrant sandal-wood.

Many jewels, and perhaps all originally, are worn as a protection against the evil influence of spirits or unlucky planets. Gems, too, are held to exercise direct beneficial influences on the wearer. Amulets of nine gems (*nau-ratan*)—zircon, cat's-eye, sapphire, diamond, ruby, pearl, coral, emerald, and topaz—are often worn as armlets or finger-rings. A pair of tiger's claws, mounted in gold or silver, and engraved with the "five weapons of Vishnu," are often worn as a talisman by Sinhalese children. Another common type of amulet consists of decorated tubes of gold or silver, to hold a written talisman, or a few drops of charmed oil; these are attached to necklaces or waist-belts, or used as armlets. Rings are not used as a sign of marriage, but there are other marks, such as a red spot on the brow, a special armlet, or a special form of bead worn round the neck (*tāli*), indicative of the married woman, serving the same purpose as a wedding-ring.

Necklaces and rosaries of *Eleocarpus* seeds (*Rudr-āksha-māla*) are worn by Shaivite priests, usually with one large double gold bead ("*Gaurī Shankar*"), in the centre. An example made in Ceylon is shown in fig. 128, completely covered with minute mythological figures in high relief. Simpler necklaces of all kinds of seeds and beads are worn everywhere.

With jewellery must be reckoned the many sorts of glass or lac, or ivory or shell bracelets worn in profusion by women of all classes, beside others of gold and gems. Nearly all Indian bangles, of whatever material, are stiff, and always as small as can possibly be squeezed over the hand. All these are broken on the death of a husband. What unsuspected romance can attach to a woman's bracelet is seen in the Rājput custom of "*rakhī*-gift." A bracelet—not necessarily valuable—may be sent by any maiden or wife, on occasion of urgent need or danger, to a man of her choice. He becomes her "bracelet-bound brother," and owes her all the devotion and service that knight could render. The chosen brother returns a *kuchlī* or bodice in token of acceptance of the pledge. But no tangible reward can ever be his, though he may risk life and kingdom on her behalf; for he may never behold her, who must remain for ever unknown to him, as to all other men, save her husband and near relations.

Perhaps the most beautiful of all Indian jewellery is that of Jaffna in Ceylon. Here, and in Southern

India, we meet with a great variety of gold chains, very light in weight and very rich in their effect. The beads are always hollow; sometimes shaped like seeds or fruits, sometimes spherical and made of wires and grains (fig. 121). The clasps, decorated in the same way with wire and pip, are unsurpassed for beauty of design and workmanship (fig. 120). Beside this art of filigree there is the very important method known as "gold-embedding" (figs. 123, 129), usually applied to flat surfaces, such as those of pendants. The thin gems, usually rubies, are embedded in wax in a slender framework backed by a plain gold plate; the spaces between the gems are then filled in with soft gold, gradually moulded by the tool to form a firm narrow bezel. This is the only form of encrustation with gems that rivals or surpasses the splendour of enamel, the use of which is quite unknown in the south of India.

Another fine type of Dravidian jewellery is the beaten gold-work, on a basis of wax; the effect of solidity and richness is here again combined with small intrinsic cost and light weight. As justly remarked by Sir George Birdwood, the Hindūs "by their consummate skill and thorough knowledge and appreciation of the conventional decoration of surface, contrive to give to the least possible weight of metal, and to gems, commercially absolutely valueless, the highest possible artistic value. . . This character of Indian jewellery is in remarkable contrast with modern European jewellery, in which the object of the jeweller seems to be to bestow the least amount of work on the greatest amount of metal." Much of the refinement and splendour of Indian jewellery depends on the use of cabochon cut stones, which reveal all their colour; when, as modern fashion dictates, facetted stones are introduced, the result is immediately thin and flashy. Of few educated Indians can it now be said that they wear jewellery worth a second glance; for the modern work is all copied from the trade catalogues of Europe. Incomparably finer existing work is often ruthlessly melted down to make the more fashionable "improved jewellery" of to-day.

The Kandyan Sinhalese jewellery is closely related to Dravidian types, since the goldsmiths and designers are mostly of Indian extraction; yet it lacks the demoniac element which sometimes appears in South Indian art, and there are many local forms, such as the pepper-spike garland and peculiar rings and earrings. The finger-rings of Kandyan chiefs are remarkable for their huge size, rivalled only by the mirror thumb-rings of the Hindustān dancing-girls.

Many of the pendants are fine examples of "gold-embedding"; none exceeding in splendour the great bird, 4⅞ inches across the wings, illustrated in fig. 129; here the eyes are sapphires, the lowest row of stones and seven others are emerald or green zircon, and all the others ruby. The silver waist-chains are especially characteristic ; one kind is made of twisted wire, with a heavy clasp, another of interlocked filigree beads, the largest in the centre, and small ones on either side, the former kind being worn by men, the latter (fig. 127) by women.

The best general idea of the northern Hindū jewellery will be gathered from the *Head of Krishna*, and *A Musician* (frontispiece and fig. 71). It will be noticed that a man can wear as much jewellery as a woman, or more, and that many forms are common to both. The *sarpesh*, or jewelled aigrette, worn in the turban, belongs to men only. Krishna wears a single pearl as a nose-ring; but the musician, a large gold ring with pearls and stones. The earrings worn by both are of the sort called *karn-phūl*; but a more characteristic man's form consists of a plain gold ring, rather thin, on which are threaded two pearls and an emerald, compared by Bāna to white jasmine flowers and green leaves. Other rings, called *bīrbali*, are enamelled. No Indian finger-rings are more beautiful than those of Jaipur, which are usually both gem-set and enamelled (figs. 124, 125). The frontal pendants are most attractive; Bāna speaks of them "dancing upon her forehead and kissing her hair parting." Many of these old Hindū forms were adopted also by the Mughals.

Enamelling is essentially a Northern Indian art, and in origin probably not Indian at all. Yet it has attained such perfection as to be fairly reckoned amongst the master-crafts of India. Enamellers from Lahore were brought by Mān Singh to Jaipur in the 16th century, and even now the crude enamel is obtained in lumps from Lahore; the Hindū craftsmen of Jaipur cannot prepare the colours for themselves. No enamelling in the world is more splendid in design and pure in colour than the old Jaipur work on gold and silver plate, the sword furniture and jewellery. The Jaipur craftsmen (Hindūs) have also settled in Delhi, where are the chief jewellers' shops of all Northern India at the present day. The Jaipur enamel, like all other Indian varieties, is of the kind called *champlevé*, that is, the enamel occupies certain hollows excavated in the surface of the metal. In the best and richest work, only a narrow band of the original metal separates one colour from another. The ground colour is a delicate ivory white, against which the brilliant reds and greens stand out to great advantage. Without this white background the effect is far less harmonious. One of the finest old examples is a scent-spray in the possession of Seth Narottam Goculdass of Bombay; there are other splendid pieces in the English and many of the Rājput royal collections, especially Jaipur and Chambā, and in the Museum at South Kensington; an armlet with representations of Rāma, Lakshmī, Sītā, and Hanuman, is illustrated in fig. 126. Though the modern work is technically and in colour almost equal to the old, it is no longer applied to serious purposes, but rather to trivial ornaments and trinkets which delight the tourist.

141. Carved ship. Stone. 8 c. Borōbodur, Jāva. Height of relief 3 ft. 3⅜ in.
142. Balcony and windows. Wood. 18 c. Gūjarāt.
143. Entrance to a house. Wood. 18 c. Lahore.

CHAPTER SIXTH   WOODWORK

EXCEPT FOR STOOLS AND BEDS, THE
Indians scarcely use furniture. They have, on the
other hand, everywhere excelled in the architectural
applications of woodwork, and until quite recently
in shipbuilding. All Indian architecture was once
wooden, and even where this is not still the case, the
wooden forms survive in stone. The workers in wood
and stone are of one and the same caste. Except in
a few places where stone abounds (*e.g.* Jaipur, Gwaliar) domestic architecture has remained wooden to
this day ; very striking work in local styles may be
seen in Ceylon, Southern India, Gūjarāt, Kāthiāwār,
Nepāl, Kāshmīr, and the Himālayas generally. The
carpenter is thus essentially an architect, as appears
already in the *Alīnachitta Jātaka*, which describes
a village of 500 carpenters who made their living by
going to the up-Ganges forests to cut the framework
of one- and two-story houses, and returning down-
stream to erect the houses thus prepared in villages
along the banks. Even when stone came into more
general use, it was largely in the form of pillars on
the ground floor, supporting a wood-framed building
above. Roofing was often highly elaborated, both
in structure and ornament, with carved rafters or
beautiful pendants. The oldest known remains of
Indian woodwork is the framing at the entrance to

could be more degraded than the popular Kāshmīr walnut tables, of which the surface is covered with realistic *chenār* leaves so deeply undercut as to make the table absolutely useless as a table.

Perforated windows are everywhere highly characteristic, as in all Oriental countries where it is desired to admit light and air without destroying privacy. The southern forms (figs. 145, 146) are usually of solid wood, perforated with designs that are more often floral than geometrical, and also include animal and figure subjects. Northern windows and balcony screens, especially in the Panjāb and Kāshmīr, are made of many small pieces of wood dowelled together, and so well fitted that even when the frame is removed they do not fall apart. These geometrical forms, called *pinjra*, have a markedly Arabic character, reminiscent of Cairo (fig. 142); but old Dravidian and Chalukyan stonework shows that built-up *jālis* of this kind are also indigenous in the south (fig. 88). Ceylon windows are either just like doors, with solid leaves fitted into a wooden frame, or consists of framed openings fitted with turned wooden pillars. Kāshmīr is noted for its geometric panelled ceilings in pine, admirably fitted and often beautifully painted. All over India, indeed, it is usual for woodwork to be more or less freely coloured, and the same is true of much of the stone-carving under cover. The subject of wood inlay is dealt with in another chapter.

Amongst the most important old structures in wood were bridges, of which the seven spanning the river Jhelam at Srinagar are striking examples, built up of huge logs laid horizontally and able to resist the heavy spring floods. Several bridges are recorded in the old Ceylon chronicles; one is described as "of exceeding great beauty, that could be passed by elephants and horses and chariots and footmen."

It is not generally realised that India has been a country of great maritime enterprise, and that much of her overseas trade has been carried in vessels of local construction. Ships are mentioned even in the *Rig-Veda* and constantly in the later literature, especially in the *Jātakas*; there are also *Shilpashāstras* in which their forms and purposes are described in detail. The Ceylon chronicles speak of ships carrying as many as 800 passengers, and some are mentioned in the *Jātakas* carrying 500 cart-loads of goods, and 800 cubits in length. From the earliest stone sculptures onwards there are many representations of ships in Indian art; they have figure-heads of all kinds of animals and birds.

The greatest period of Indian shipbuilding, however, must have been the Imperial age of the Guptas

166

and Harshavardhana, when the Indians possessed
great colonies in Pegu, Cambodia, Jāva, Sumat-
ra, and Borneo, and trading settlements in China,
Japan, Arabia, and Persia. Amongst the Javanese
sculptures there are many representations of ships,
showing their framing, and noticeable for the outriggers, necessitated by their narrow and top-heavy
build (fig. 141). These outriggers are still characteristic of the beautiful Ceylon fishing-boats; and
when much sail is carried, some of the crew climb out
on to them.

Many notices in the works of European traders
and adventurers in the 15th and 16th centuries show
that the Indian ships of that day were larger than
their own; Purchas, for example, mentions one met
by a Captain Saris in the Red Sea, of 1200 tons
burden, about three times the size of the largest
English ships then made (1611).

Another important kind of carpentry is exemplified in the very varied cars and chariots, from those
of the gods and kings, down to the heavy country
carts with almost solid wheels drawn by white oxen,
and the light Ceylon "hackeries" drawn by racing
bulls. Representations of all these types are common in the sculpture and painting. The cars of the
gods in which the images are carried in procession

on holydays are most elaborate structures literally covered with mythological carvings. They are usually drawn by elephants or by hundreds of men pulling long ropes. Accidents which have taken place at Purī have given rise to the myth of the "car of Juggernaut" (Jagannātha, "Lord of the World"), beneath the wheels of which the pilgrim devotees were supposed to throw themselves.

Chairs and thrones have been always familiar to Indians, but were used only by kings; others, according to their rank, sat on low stools or on the ground. The stools are either of cane, shaped like an hour-glass, a form from which a typical pedestal of metal and stone images has been derived, or of wood, and three-legged or four-legged (*chaukī*). But furniture forms a most unimportant element in the Indian culture, where all the ordinary business of life is conducted on the ground; in an ordinary house, for instance, there will be found but empty rooms, the floor covered with a cotton *darī* or cloth, and provided with big cylindrical cushions; and only perhaps when meals are served will a small stool, a few inches high, be used. But it is not infrequent for such a house to be also provided with a swing or seat suspended from the ceiling; the same method is adopted for cradles. Beds (*chārpai*) are four-legged, strung with rattan or webbing; the legs assume architectural forms, or may be turned, and are then often painted or lacquered. Some of the best wood-carving is to be found in the low headpieces morticed into the bed-legs which project above the frame (fig. 144). Nevertheless, everyone is well accustomed to sleep quite comfortably on the ground or a hard bench. Almost all modern Indian furniture intended for European use is bad in design, workmanship, and decoration ; but there existed in the 17th century in the west and south, including Ceylon, a good "Indo-Portuguese" style, especially well illustrated in the great wooden chests, with handsome brass fittings. Indian carpenters, as in the case of so many of the other crafts, can still do admirable work, when they are asked to do so and when they are properly paid.

Of all Indian carpenters' work, perhaps the most admirable appears in the making of musical instruments. It would be impossible to improve on the perfection of form and appropriate decoration of the Tanjore *tamburas* and *vīnās*, as they are even now made, while there is scarcely any part of India where clever instrument makers cannot still be discovered. The great age of Indian music was probably as long ago as the 5th century A.D. : but many instruments were in use long before that, of forms similar to those now seen. In particular, the *vīnā* is the classic solo instrument of Hindū culture, carried always by Sarasvatī, goddess of learning and science, and by the *rishi* Nārada and by various *rāginis* (fig. 78.) The *tambura* is used solely as an accompaniment to song, and, like the *vīnā*, often represented in the Rājput drawings (fig. 74). Next in importance to these are the several kinds of drums.

Quite an important craft is that of inlaying wood with metal, usually brass. The best example of this is the *tar-kāshi* or wire-inlay of Mainpuri and elsewhere in Bengal. The work is done on hard black *shisham* wood; the elaborate geometrical design is first incised, then the flat wire laid and hammered into the incisions, while the innumerable dots and points are minute coils of wire twisted up on the point of a needle, and inserted in small punched holes; the surface is subsequently filed over and polished. The objects to which this sort of decoration was formerly applied included wooden clogs for bathers, pen-cases, Koran-stands, kitchen rollers, and the like; now it is used chiefly for photo-frames and work-boxes; and, more satisfactorily, for the decoration of doors, of which there are good examples in the town hall of Bulandshahr. Good work is also done at Chinniot and elsewhere in the Panjāb, where

WOODWORK

the art originated in the decoration of camel-panni-
ers, but is now chiefly applied to screens. Here, as
also in Calcutta, the inlay is not confined to wire, but
includes larger plates of metal.

Ivory inlaying and marquetry are described in the
chapters on "Ivory" and "Minor Mughal Crafts."

Wood block for *chikan* embroidery, Lucknow, 20th century.

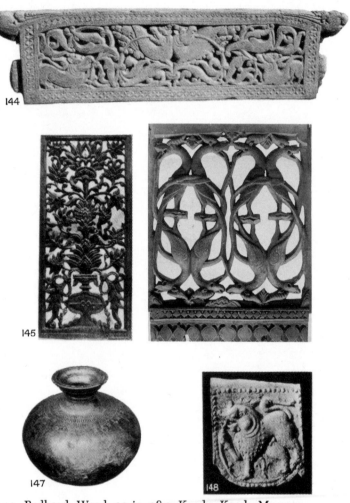

144. Bedhead. Wood. 30 in. 18 c. Kandy. Kandy Museum.
145. Window. Wood. 18 c. Malabar. Captain Welch.
146. Perforated window. Wood. Four pairs of dragon-headed birds. Madras. 18 c. Museum of Fine Arts, Boston.
147. Water-carrying vessel. Earthenware. Stamped ornament, well-developed shoulder. 18-19 c. Kandy. Kandy Museum.
148. Eaves-tile. Earthenware. Moulded by pressure, hollow space between. (Small hole in the *hamsa* permits expansion of air during firing of tile.) Dāladā Māligāva. 6½ in. 18-19 c. Kandy, Sinhalese. Museum of Fine Arts, Boston.

flourishing Indian arts from early times. Unfortunately, however, there does not exist a single example
of very ancient work, unless we reckon the terra-cotta medallion of fig. 18, which is almost certainly the
impression of an ivory die. This is of the 2nd century
B.C., like the Sānchī gates and Bharhut railing, and in
a similar style, only finer in workmanship. The ivory
chessmen found at Brāhmanabād, Sind, may be of the
8th century A.D. The inlaid doorways of the Ashar
Mahall at Bījāpur (Musulmān) were made in 1580.

Buddhist Ceylon is far the richest source for later
work, some of which must be as old as the 15th century. There are very fine collections in the Colombo
Museum and at South Kensington. The Sinhalese
traditions are closely related to those of Travancore, and preserve old Indian motifs, generally similar to those of Chalukyan stone-carving, rather than
modern Dravidian forms. An enumeration of objects
from the Kandyan provinces of Ceylon will give an
idea of the varied applications: there are images of
Buddha and other statuettes and dolls; architectural
applications, especially to the jambs and lintels of
vihāra doorways (fig. 135); handles of daggers and
knives, and of water-dippers (of which there is a fine
example at South Kensington); combs; boxes made
of carved plaques connected by metal fittings (fig.

136); book-covers; compasses (fig. 133); guards of fencing-foils; potters' dies—all carved; and of turned work, many sorts of boxes, fan handles, knife handles, dice and pawns for games; scent-sprays (hollow, and so thin as to be easily compressible); drums, book-buttons, and still other forms. The best carvings in low relief are the figures of guardian *devatās* (fig. 134) placed on either side of the threshold of *vihāra* doors; while many of the combs are of admirable workmanship and design. Horn is put to similar uses, the chief objects being combs, pill-boxes, and powder horns. The combs and pill-boxes are occasionally inlaid with ivory pegs, or coloured lac; the powder horns are carved or mounted in silver.

Much more artistic than the rather stiff ivory statuettes of 18th-century Ceylon are certain works from Nayagarh in Orissa, made by Gobind Ratan about 1850. These have been often illustrated, and deservedly praised; one, a figure of Krishna, with rich and detailed ornament, is shown in fig. 132.

There are many forms of ivory inlay or marquetry, and appliqué. There still remain good examples of the latter in the palace at Tanjore, from which so many treasures of art have been taken away. There is a small car, with ivory rails and overlaid with ivory plaques, of which a part is illustrated in fig. 138. Two chairs veneered with ivory well exemplify the method of further decoration with coloured lac (fig. 137). In this most effective work the surface of the ivory is first engraved, then coloured lac is run into the incisions by means of a hot bolt, and finally the surface is scraped and polished, leaving a clear design in black, red, or green on the ivory ground. The method is nowhere more successfully applied than in the decoration of the beautiful musical instruments (*vīnā* and *tambura*) which are still made by the Tanjore carpenters. A still more important centre for veneered ivory is Vizagapatam, where the style of carving is low and flat, and ivory-staining as well as lac-inlay is also practised; the Tanjore and Vizagapatam styles are thus closely related. The same technique is practised in Mysore and at Mātara in Ceylon, where the design is usually in black. In Kandy, and in Rājputāna, turned ivory boxes and other lathe-works are decorated with simpler motifs, lines, circles, and dots. Lac-inlay is also applied to the ornamenting of shell or ivory bracelets in several localities, and to shell trumpets (*sankh*), of which a fine example is illustrated from Ceylon (fig. 140).

The Travancore ivories, which closely resemble those of Ceylon, are represented by the fine casket of fig. 136 at South Kensington; the dancing figures

178

could be exactly paralleled from old sculptures. Some of the most modern Travancore ivory, of which examples were shown at the great Delhi Exhibition in 1902–3, is equal in design and workmanship to almost any old work. This purity of design was especially shown in a money-counting board, with holes for a hundred small coins, and a handle of addorsed leogriffs and floriated ornament. Images in the round, shrines, and other large works are also produced. It is interesting to contrast this purity of feeling preserved in Travancore work with the degeneration in design characteristic of Mysore and Ceylon. In Mysore the conventional designs have been replaced by realistic jungle scenes, which aim rather at pictorial than decorative qualities,* while in Ceylon,

---

* I cannot resist quoting here a description from the Delhi catalogue: An ivory brush-back "portrays gracefully every feature of jungle life and sport. The foreground, distance, and clouds are all faithfully treated, and, in a manner that is most surprising, every detail is shown, and still the atmosphere of high-class painting has not been materially disturbed, nor the picture overburdened" (Sir George Watt, *Indian Art at Delhi*). The reader may be interested in a few more criticisms originating in the "atmosphere of high-class painting." The present Principal of the Calcutta School of Art dismisses the painting of Ajantā as "more decorative than pictorial, so that it can hardly be classed among the fine arts" (*loc. cit.*). Another art-school master (Bombay), has lamented the "massive proportions and primitive character of Indian jewellery." The author of the only systematic *History of Fine Art in India and Ceylon*, wrote only five years ago that "after

though old motifs are retained, the whole energy of the carver is devoted to obtaining rounded forms and deep undercutting, producing costly works in poor taste. Only the ivory-turning of Ceylon survives as good as ever, though on a small scale, and on the verge of disappearing from lack of demand.

The older Mysore ivories are truly magnificent, especially a chair-back of the 17th century, consisting of pierced tree and animal panels, surmounted by a design of twisting monsters, not unlike the wooden bed-head from Ceylon illustrated in fig. 144. Mysore is also a centre of ivory inlay and inlay of black lac, said to be superior to any of the better known work of the Panjāb; and of the greater part of the trade in carved sandal-wood.

The architectural uses of ivory are usually confined to the decoration of doors, of which a fine example from Ceylon has already been referred to. At Bikaner, in the old palace, there are wooden doors

300 A.D. Indian sculpture, properly so called, hardly deserves to be reckoned as art." (It is fair to add that this view has since been modified.) Sir George Birdwood has compared some of the finest Buddha sculptures to a boiled suet pudding. Baden-Powell, writing of the arts of the Panjāb (including Kāngrā), remarks : " In a country like this *we must not expect* to find anything that appeals to mind or deep feeling" (italics mine). These quotations will serve to show what sort of " experts " have had to do with the study of Indian art, and with the artistic education offered to young Indians.

of which the leaves are covered with a raised net-
work of ivory appliqué, but this northern art is not,
as in the south, pure old Hindū, but more than half
Mughal. There are doors veneered with ivory in the
palace at Amber, and in the Barī Mahall at Udaipur, where there also used to be made quantities of
beautifully decorated ivory thumb-guards for archers. Jodhpur is the centre of a trade in ivory bangles,
ink-green and black lac.

Ivory inlay on wood is a characteristic art of the
Panjāb. The best examples are the inlaid doors of
the main entrance to the Golden Temple at Amritsar. At Jalandhar and Hoshiarpur it has also been
a flourishing craft, especially in its application to the
decoration of musical instruments, and to other serious ends; but now if one inquires from a Jalandhar
craftsman what such and such an article in his shop
may be for, he will answer, "To put on the mantel-
piece."

The ivory work of Murshīdābād in Bengal consists of objects for the tourist trade, and images of
Durgā for the local market, all in a thin and flimsy
style and quite modern.

The better-known work of Delhi is almost equally
modern, and though in Brāhman hands, has grown
up almost entirely in response to tourist demands.

A favourite subject is an elephant loaded with guns, camp furniture, etc., each article attached by a chain cut from the solid ivory, each link not bigger than a pin's head. The work has scarcely any artistic merit.

It is worth while to remark that a good deal of the material used for dagger-handles and similar purposes is not Indian or African ivory, but is known as "fish-tooth," most of it being really fossil ivory from Siberia. Old examples prove that there used to exist an overland trade in this material. Hippopotamus and walrus ivory may also have found its way to India by land routes. It is remarkable how little the question of distance from a source of raw material, or from a market, appears to affect an old manufacture, as, for example, in the cases of the Masulipatam cotton printing still done for the Persian market, shell-work at Dacca, far from the sea, and ebony-carving at Nagina, far from any forests where ebony grows. Many of these now isolated industries are survivals of more widely extended crafts, and it is clear that communications in ancient India, if not as rapid, were scarcely less free than they are now.

An adequate history of Indian work in ivory still remains to be written, and perhaps no other craft would throw more light on the history and migrations of designs in India than this.

149. Embroidered cloth. Silk on cotton. Chambā. 18-19 c. Lahore Museum.
150. Embroidered sari (*chikan* work). Cotton on muslin. Lucknow.
151. Embroidery, detail (*phulkāri*). Each unit 3¾ in. Silk on cotton. Panjāb. Author.
152. Embroidered shield-cushion (detail). 1¾ in. Silk on cotton. Jaipur. Author.

CHAPTER EIGHTH
STONE, EARTHENWARE, GESSO, LAC

AT A VERY EARLY DATE THE HINDŪS possessed great skill in polishing and piercing the hardest gems; beads of ruby and sapphire are to be seen in all collections. There are also a few important examples of engraved seals. Perhaps the most remarkable ancient Hindū work in stone is the unique jade tor-

Jade tortoise from Allahābād.

toise, 17½ inches long, from Allahābād, now in the British Museum; or can this work be of Chinese origin?

The best known of the old works in crystal are the relic shrines which have been found in many *stūpas*. Of much later date are the fine stock-drill weights and sandal grinding-stones of Ceylon. The modern turned soapstone cups and platters of Calcutta are of very elegant forms, which, were they antique, would attract much attention.

Nothing like china has ever been made in India. Even glazed pottery, previous to the Musulmān tile-work, occurs quite exceptionally and sporadically (Peshāwar, Anurādhapura, Gwaliar, Vellore). The modern glazed pottery of Multān, Jaipur, and Bombay is a recent development of Musulmān tile-craft, mainly for tourist consumption. The unglazed earthenware, on the contrary, all over India, is of the remotest antiquity, in form and technique unaltered since prehistoric times. The forms are of exceptional simplicity and dignity, while the decorative ornament, especially in Ceylon, is of great interest as preserving many archaic (Mykenean or Early Asiatic) motifs. Few types are designed for purposes of eating or drinking, for an earthen vessel thus once used is defiled, and must be thrown away; the Hindūs invariably eat from leaves, or brass or silver or stone vessels which can be perfectly cleansed.

The most usual forms are designed for carrying water (fig. 147), and for storing grain, spices, and even clothing. The Sinhalese types have been studied in most detail; beside those already mentioned, there are several interesting forms of architectural earthenware, such as tiles (plain roofing tiles and eaves tiles decorated with lions, etc., fig. 148), finials, and lamps and lampstands. The methods of decoration are also

of much interest, and include slip-painting and incised or stamped ornament. The incised ornament
is of an exceedingly archaic type; while the stamped
pattern most frequently seen is the pointed *bo*-leaf.
Pottery painting is the work of painters, not of those
who make the pots.

In Southern India it has been customary from time
immemorial to construct large earthenware animals
and figures of men and gods, which are placed in
sacred groves near human dwellings—a survival of
primitive sculpture in impermanent materials. Similar forms are extensively used in the decoration of
temples. The terra-cotta figures of Lucknow have
already been mentioned. Amongst the most frequent finds on old Buddhist sites are baked terra-
cotta impressions of seals, usually with the representation of a stūpa, and with inscriptions. The oldest
and most beautiful of the terra-cotta medallions is
illustrated from a drawing in fig. 18. Ancient baked
earthenware hand-blocks for cotton printing are also
known.

Many parts of India are noted for fine work in
stucco, carved just before it sets. Walls are also coated with exceedingly fine and hard white cement; the
inner wall of the gallery at Sīgiriya, in Ceylon, for
example, remains as smooth to-day as when it was

finished fourteen hundred years ago, though exposed to rain and air : even the names scribbled on it so long ago are still clearly legible.

Of similar character, but generally more trivial application, is the art of ornamenting wooden and other surfaces with *gesso*. Here the moulding material is applied with a brush, like paint, and subsequently varnished, gilded, or painted. Bikaner, Tonk, Hyderābād, and the Karnul district are the chief centres.

Lac-work is quite distinct in character from Japanese lacquer, inasmuch as the lac is not applied with a brush, but in a solid or half-melted form. In India it is applied mainly to turned woodwork, the stick of coloured lac being held against the revolving wood, and adhering by the heat of friction. Brightly coloured toys, nests of boxes, and bed-legs are thus made in many districts. Not infrequently, and especially in Jaipur, Hoshiarpur, and the Maldive Islands, a coating of several layers of lac of different colours is thus laid on, and then incised to corresponding depths, so as to show a pattern in various colours. A thin layer of lac is also sometimes used, in Sind and in Ceylon, as a protection for a water-colour under-painting. More peculiar is the finger-nail work of Ceylon, in which the coloured lac is drawn out into long threads and applied to a warm surface, to

LAC

make quite elaborate patterns. In this case the form of the surface to be decorated may be either flat or cylindrical. The thumb-nail is used to nip off each piece of lac thread applied, hence the name.

Engraved bull, from a copper-plate grant : Silahara, 11th century A.D.

153. Part of brocaded belt (*patiya*). Cotton. Width, 8½ in. Ūva,
 Ceylon. Kandy.
154. Cotton quilt, or mat (*etirila*). Cotton. 20 c. Kandy. Author.
155. Brocade. Gold thread on silk. Tanjore. 20 c. Author.
156. Hanging. Cotton printed. 18 c. Museum of Fine Arts, Boston.
157. Detail of embroidered skirt. Silk on satin. Sind. 18-19 c.
 Author.

CHAPTER NINTH   TEXTILES, EMBROIDERY, COSTUME,   &c.

WEAVING IS AT ONCE THE OLDEST and the most important of the industrial arts of India. The stuffs may be considered from the standpoint of material and use, and then of decoration, either on the loom (tapestry, brocade, etc.) or after removal from the loom (dyeing, printing, embroidery, etc.). All of these arts have a rich and wide development in India and Persia; the materials exported from these countries for at least three thousand years past have been the main vehicle of Asiatic influence on Western arts (Crete, Ionia, Sicily, the Crusades, Venice, East India Company, etc.).

The great majority of Indians wear cotton garments, and it is from India that all such names as *chintz, calico, shawl,* and *bandana* have come into English since the 18th century. Weaving is frequently mentioned in the *Vedas,* and cotton, silk, and woollen stuffs in the epics. Silk was certainly imported from China as early as the 4th century B.C., but it is probable that no industry was established until very much later. Megasthenes describes the cotton garments of the Indians as "worked in gold and ornamented with various stones," and, he says, "they wear also flowered garments of the finest muslin,' —such as are still made at Dacca. The old sculp-

193

tures and paintings show brocaded materials, as well as muslins so filmy and transparent that only the lines of the borders or the folds show that the figures are clothed at all. The robes are usually woven in the shape and size required for use, and only rarely and locally cut into fitting garments, so that tailoring (apart from embroidery) is a comparatively unimportant craft.

The typical garments of uncut woven stuff are, for men, the *dhoti* (like a divided skirt, from the waist to below the knees), a shawl or scarf, and a turban (*pagrī*, *sāfa*); for women, a *sārī* (worn rather like a *dhoti*, but brought over one or both shoulders, and sometimes over the head also), with or without a bodice. This is the usual dress from Bengal and Bombay southwards, and for some purposes, especially any religious observance, also in Rājputāna and the Panjāb. In the latter areas, however, the outdoor and usual costume of Hindū men consists of trousers, tunic (*kurta*), coat (*choga*, etc.), and turban; and of women, striped trousers, full skirt, bodice (*cholī*), or tunic (*kurta*), and veil (*dupatta*, *chadar*). Details vary from district to district and village to village; the form of the turban always serving to distinguish the men of one place from those of any other. The Bengālīs, however, wear small embroidered white caps, and no turbans. The use of trousers and long coats is not ancient Indian; but it goes much further back than the Mughal period, and may be of Greeko-Bactrian or Hūna origin. A turban piece may be 3 yards square, as in the south; 30 yards by 1, as in the Panjāb; or in some places still longer and narrower; a *dhoti* averages 5 yards by $1\frac{1}{4}$, and a *sārī* 5 to 8 yards by $1\frac{1}{4}$. Needless to remark, there is much art in wearing garments which are not fastened by any stitch, pin, or knot.

Cotton-weaving is the typical textile industry of India. It must have been once a true domestic industry (as it is to this day in Assam), practised even by ladies of rank, or at least as a part of the household work; but in most parts of India weaving, like embroidery, was already in Buddhist times a distinct profession, and carried on largely, though not exclusively, by men. The Indian loom is horizontal, the heddles being operated by the weaver's feet. Quite plain material was at one time produced everywhere, and there are still perhaps as many as five million hand weavers in India. To give some idea of local styles, we may refer more especially to Dacca in Bengal and the Kandyan provinces in Ceylon. The former locality is noted for its muslins, which represent the highest development of pure cotton-weaving in India. The fine muslins have received poetic names, such as "running water," "woven air," and "evening dew," the last because the muslin, laid on wet grass, could hardly be seen. Pieces of 15 yards by 1 have been produced weighing only 900 grains; the finest yarn may be worth as much as £3, 3s. an ounce. Muslins are still made up to as much as £4 a yard. But it is not only for very fine plain material, but also for flowered muslins, that Bengal is famous; they are still much worn by the ladies of Bengal, those, at least, who have the good taste to avoid the corsets and blouses of Europe.

The flowered muslins are loom-tapestries; that is to say, the substance of the cloth is shuttle-work, but the patterns, usually small flower-sprays *semé*, are inserted by hand as the work proceeds, a tiny bobbin or "needle" of the coloured or gold thread being passed through and round the warp threads in the manner of tapestry.

The Sinhalese cotton was of very different quality; no muslin was made, but the best stuffs were thick, soft, and heavy like the finest linen. The craft is preserved in only one village. There are many simple traditional designs, some geometrical, others of flowers, animals, or very elaborate strap-work, like that in Keltic manuscripts, or such as one sees at

is worked out in raised nails or pins, which push up the material in the same pattern. The cloth is next lifted off, and the raised portions caught by the thumb and forefinger nails of the girls who do the work, and securely tied by a string, usually coated with a resist paste. The thread is not cut, but passes from knot to knot, and can afterwards be unwound and used again. After the first knotting, the cloth is dyed. Then the process is repeated for another part of the pattern, and the cloth dyed again. Finally, when the thread is unwound and the cloth spread out, the required design appears in dots of various colours on a ground of the colour in which the material is last immersed. For example, we may have a red field with white and yellow points, or a black field with white, yellow, and red points, in the first case with two tyings, in the second with three. There are even greater complications, *e.g.* when large white patches or stars are left white through several dippings, and then treated separately with other colours. In many cases the raised block is dispensed with altogether, and the tyer "will work rapidly and outline a bird, a horseman, or a flower, and pass over certain points in the design that require to be tied at subsequent stages, while carrying on a heated controversy with a neighbour or attending to her infant child" (Watt).

By a somewhat similar process the Marwārī turbans and *chadars* are dyed in chevron and zigzag patterns of the utmost complexity. Another peculiar art of the Rājput dyers (Alwar, etc.) is double-dyeing, where muslin is coloured differently on the two sides of the piece.

While tie-dyeing is quite a local craft, cotton-printing and dye-painting are widely spread; in these ancient crafts the beauty of design and colouring and fastness of dye are alike remarkable. The cotton prints are the originals of all the prints and chintzes now familiar in Europe. The best work of comparatively recent times has been done in the United Provinces (Lucknow, etc.), the Panjāb (Lahore), Rājputāna (Sānganīr), and other places; also in Southern India, where dye-painting is an equally important craft. But in most districts these crafts are now either quite degenerate in quality, or greatly reduced in prosperity, by the competition of cheap and inferior European factory goods and the wholesale piracy of Indian designs.

The designs are printed by hand from wood blocks, a separate block being necessary for each colour. The block-printed area is covered with a resist paste if the ground is to be dyed. Favourite motifs are the cone or shawl-pattern (as fig. 195), widespread from north to south, flower-sprays (*būtis*) of every sort arranged over the ground diagonally, diapers, birds (especially peacocks), and continuous floral border patterns (*bēl*).

Impression of a wood block for cotton-printing, Madras.

Fine curtains and dados are still made at Lahore, one of the very few instances where a school of art has revived or preserved an indigenous industry without destroying its character.

Two examples of printing blocks are illustrated here, one of an elephant from Madras, the other taken from an earthenware block anterior to the 5th century A.D. from the Bannu district, N.W.P.

The prevailing colours in the dye-painted cloths of Masulipatam, where a small industry survives from the earliest times, still producing goods almost equal to the finest old work, are blue (indigo) and red (madder), with green, yellow, and black on an ivory-white ground.

Earthenware printing block, Bannu district, anterior to 5th century. Collection of Mr Longworth Dames.

The favourite designs are the tree of life, and panels in the form of Saracenic doorways. There is still an export trade in dyed cottons from Masulipatam to Persia. The methods are as follows: to obtain a design, let us say, in yellow on red, the whole is first dyed yellow, then the desired pattern is drawn in hot beeswax with a soft steel wire brush, then the whole is dipped in red. Where the wax penetrates the cloth, it is completely protected from the red dye, so that when it is afterwards boiled out the pattern appears in yellow on red. In the same way, by repeated waxings and dyeings, a very complex design can be prepared in several colours. Large areas may also be separately brush-coloured, or partly or wholly printed from wood-blocks. Very often the large hand-painted palampores are prepared for colouring by pouncing the design through pricked paper stencil plates.

The Masulipatam designs are of a Persian character. But from Kalahastri, Karnapur, Pallakallo, and other South Indian centres there come hand-painted cloths of purely Hindū design. The most striking are those covered with mythological subjects, or scenes from the epics, intended for ceiling cloths to be used in temples, or for covering processional cars.

Neither cotton-printing nor dye-painting are Sinhalese crafts. All the finer cloths found in Ceylon appear to be of Indian origin. There is evidence of several settlements of Indian weavers in Ceylon on various occasions.

Embroidery is an important craft, for the most part, but not entirely in the hands of professional workers, who are usually men. We may take as typical localities for well-marked styles, Ceylon, Lucknow, Rājputāna, and the Panjāb. It is often

quite a folk-art, used to decorate the garments even
of those who work in the fields; and the local forms
are very clearly marked.

The Ceylon work is almost exclusively in cotton,
in red, blue, or white, on a blue or white ground.
Fairly elaborate figure-work in chain-stitch is characteristic of some of the large betel-bags, while *bō-*
leaf, lotus-petal, and continuous floral motifs appear
in the borders. Chain and button-hole stitch are
most frequent, while there is a considerable variety
of binding stitches for edges, one of which (the "cen-
tipede") is extremely complicated, and worked in
two or three colours. Small handkerchiefs are sometimes worked in elaborate strap-patterns, alike on
both sides, similar to those of the woven stuffs. Other
things embroidered are flags, caps, short jackets, and
pachīsi-cloths. Very elegant plaited cords and tas-
sels are prepared, the former for book-strings, the
latter for the betel-bags. The work was mostly done
by washermen ; more elaborate processional fans,
trappings, and hats were made by the court tailors.
Practically nothing of the craft now survives.

Appliqué work is done everywhere; examples are
tent-linings, cart-covers, and elephant trappings.

Kāthiāwār and Kach are most important centres
of chain-stitch embroidery. The most characteristic

work is seen on the old satin skirts (fig. 157), embroidered in the most brilliant silks with sprays of flowers and borders of flowers and birds, usually parrots. Many parts of Rājputāna and the Panjāb are also noteworthy for embroidered bodices. A very common feature in all work of this class is the inclusion of innumerable small discs of mirror glass forming part of the embroidered design, and held down in a circle of button-hole stitching. Sometimes the amount of glass is such as to make the material uncomfortably heavy. There is also much peasant work in satin-stitch, the material being often completely concealed by the floss-silk embroidery.

It is noteworthy that in Gūjarāt and Bombay one meets with a large amount of old and modern Chinese needlework, on *sārī* borders and jackets evidently prepared in China for the Indian market. It is quite possible that much of the Chinese influence recognisable here and there in Rājput art can be attributed to communications by sea.

Very fine chain-stitch embroideries (silk on cotton) are found in Jaipur; some of these are of Musulmān design (prayer mats, etc.), but the most striking are the small square cushions (*gaddis*) used for protecting the knuckles from contact with the interior of the shield. The subjects are Hindū—mythological, floral, geometrical designs, and animal combats (fig. 152). Woollen *chadars* embroidered in cross-stitch, very like old English samplers in design, are made by the peasant women of Hissar and Bikaner. These last involve a process of counting threads of the ground material, which is much further developed in the typical Panjāb *phulkārīs*, or flowered *chadars* or women's head-veils. The work is almost entirely in silk on a red cotton ground, or red and green on white; but it is likely that the embroidery itself was once entirely in cottons, when silk was unknown or too rare for common use. The perfection of the work depends on absolute accuracy of thread-counting, as the ground itself forms part of the design (fig. 151). The stitch is a pure darning stitch, done from the back. The original art belongs to the Hindū peasants (*jāts*) of Rohtak, Gurgaon, and Delhi; while a more elaborate development, no longer for peasant use, is found in the Hazāra district, where the same classes have been converted to Islam. The craft is thus distinctively Hindū in character. The Hazāra work is no longer *phulkārī* (flowered), but *bāgh* (garden), almost completely covered with work; the outlining of the elements of the geometrical design may be effected by a residuum of ground of only $\frac{1}{16}$ inch in width. The normal stitch is about ¼-inch in length, but this rises to as much as 2 inches in the gaudy monstrosities now prepared for American and English tourists.

A quite different sort of work (fig. 149) is seen in the well-known Chambā *rumals* (square handkerchiefs or small shawls) ; this is again a home industry, and for local use. The designs are borrowed from the Pahārī paintings, and are outlined with a brush in Indian ink before the needlework is begun. There are also geometrical designs of a sampler fashion ; the material is cotton, the work silk satin-stitch.

A very different art is the white embroidery called *chikan* (fig. 150). It is probable that the craft originated in Eastern Bengal, and it is seen also in Bhopal, Madras, and other places; but Lucknow is the great modern centre, where work is done of quite remarkable beauty and distinction, and as good as any ever produced. The designs are printed from wood blocks, of which the chief employers possess an enormous stock. These blocks in themselves are of much interest, for the excellence of their design and workmanship, suggesting how easily an art of wood-engraved illustration for printed books might have grown up under more fortunate artistic auspices than those which have attended the beginnings of

206

Indian printing.*

Much of the fine *chikan* embroidery is now applied
to European purposes (blouses, dress-pieces, etc.);
but caps, *sārīs*, and *chogas* are also made for Indian
use. The following peculiarities appear in the best
Lucknow work on muslin: *taipchi* is a simple darn-
stitch used in the cheaper work; the variety called
bukhia is an inverted satin-stitch in which the forms
are merely outlined on the right side by minute stitches, while the thread accumulates beneath making
the form opaque; a similar effect is produced by very
minute appliqué called *khatao*; raised work like tiny
French knots, $\frac{1}{16}$ or $\frac{1}{32}$ inch in size, is produced by a
minute satin-stitch; lace-like trellises (*jālī*) are made,
not by drawing out threads, but by a sort of very fine
button-holing pulling the threads aside. Portions
of the work are often done in fine yellow tasar silk,
the greater part always in white cotton; in the best
examples many or all of these methods are used together. All other modern Indian embroidery is spoilt
by the use of glaring colours or too much gold, but
this white work remains of supreme excellence, comparable only with the best European lace, to which
it corresponds in purpose and effect. It may be re-

* Indian printed books are unsurpassed for badness of paper, ink,
press-work, type, and illustration.

marked here that what is commonly called "gold lace" in India, is woven stuff with gold thread. The manufacture of true lace in India is of quite modern introduction, and rarely proceeds further than the copying of European designs in inferior materials.

Wood blocks for *chikan* embroidery, Lucknow, 20th century.

A brief reference must be made to floor coverings other than woollen carpets, which are referred to in Part II. The familiar cotton *darī* is the true indigenous carpet, much cooler to the bare foot than any wool-pile rug could be. The ordinary *darīs* are striped in two colours, generally white and blue; but there are not wanting others well decorated with geometrical and even floral designs in several colours. Another important industry is the weaving of grass mats, the best of which are much more remarkable in respect of cost and beauty than might be supposed possible. The Pālghāt mats, which are quite plain except for a narrow border, are almost as fine as a Panama hat and may cost as much as £2. The *sital-pati* mats of Eastern Bengal have a high reputation. In Ceylon cheap mats of excellent design and brightly coloured are made from the fibre of bowstring hemp, woven by people of low caste on a very primitive loom ; other mats are plaited from dyed rushes in very elaborate geometrical designs by women of the higher castes, who also prepare elegant rush bags and baskets. The strongest and most beautiful grass mats in the world are probably those of the Maldive Islands, which have archaic designs in black on a khaki ground.

PART TWO
MUGHAL ART

CHAPTER TEN
ARCHITECTURE

158. Great Arch Mosque. Sandstone. 13 c. Ajmer.
159. The Kutb Mīnār. Sandstone. 14 c. Delhi.
160. Tomb of Sheikh Salīm Chishti. Marble. 16 c. Fathpur-Sīkrī.

161. Mosque of Sīdī Sayyid. Sandstone and marble. 15 c. Ahmadābād.

162. Gol Gumbāz tomb (Circular Dome). Octagonal towers eight
stories high. Sandstone. 16 c. Southwest view. Bījāpur.
(Second largest dome in the world; internal height 178 ft.)

163. Buland Darwăza (High Gate) of Jām-i Mosque, Akbar's
palace. Sandstone and marble. 16 c. Fathpur-Sīkrī.
164. Tomb of Itimād-ud-daula, near Āgra. White marble inlaid
with pietra dura and semi-precious stones. 16 c.
165. Audience Hall (Dīwān-i-khās). Sandstone. 16 c. Fathpur-
Sīkrī.

166. Bābur, laying out a garden, painting by Nahna and Bishan Dās. Late 16 c. p. of a MS. Early Mughal. Victoria and Albert Museum, Crown Copyright.

167. Man slaying a demon. Painting on cloth. Early Mughal. Victoria and Albert Museum, Crown Copyright.

168. Sultān ʿAlā-al-dīn, Fīrūz (1296-1303). Painting on paper. Mid-16 c. Early Mughal. British Museum, London.

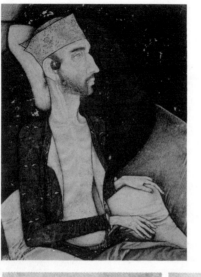

169. "Dying man." (A similar painting on paper, Death of Ināyat
   Khān, probably the same subject, to be found at the Museum
   of Fine Arts, Boston.) Painting on paper. Early 17 c. Mughal.
   Bodleian.
170. Gosain Chidrūp Yogī, by Dhan Sah. Painting on paper. Early
   17 c. Mughal. Ajmer.
171. Conversation between cobra and buffalo. Illustration to MS.
   Early 17 c. Mughal. British Museum, London.

CHAPTER TENTH   ARCHITECTURE

THE MUSULMĀN INVADERS OF INDIA, after the purely destructive period, were builders of mosques, palaces, and walled cities and forts, and tombs. The essential features of their own tradition, inherited from 9th-century Baghdad, included the dome, pointed arch, and mīnār or tower; these, in India, fused with the already existing motifs of the same character. The history of Muhammadan architecture in India begins in the 13th century, and falls into two periods, pre-Mughal (1193 to 1494) and Mughal (1494 to 1708, and later). In the first period, the local Hindū masons frequently used the remains of existing Jain or Hindū temples as their source of building materials: in the second, there is a closer fusion of foreign and indigenous tradition, creating the beautiful and very well-known architecture of the Great Mughals.

The chief monuments of the first period are the remains of the splendid 13th-century mosque at Ajmer (fig. 158), consisting of a screen of seven arches, decorated with inscriptions and arabesque ornament: the similar but even more exquisitely decorated Kutb mosque of eleven arches at Delhi, and the great Kutb mīnār (fig. 159) beside it. Both mosques are largely built of materials from older temples, and the mīnār is mainly Hindū in its details;

only the plan of all these buildings is entirely Saracenic. As Fergusson points out, the Pathāns, a nation of soldiers equipped for conquest, brought with them neither artists nor architects, and "found among their new subjects an infinite number of artists quite capable of carrying out any design that might be propounded to them." A century later is the great gateway on the south side of the Kutb mosque, where for the first time we meet with a true keyed arch.

To the 15th century belongs the important local style of the Sharqī kings of Jaunpur. Here the great gateways and the halls have radiating arches and true domes, but Hindū construction and design remain in the smaller galleries and cloisters. Bengal exhibits another provincial style typically of brick construction and characterised by its heavy short pillars and the constant use of the overhanging curved cornice. The most beautiful example of the Bengālī style is the small Golden Mosque at Gaur (*ca.* 1500).

The pre-Mughal Muhammadan architecture of Gūjarāt, in the local Hindū and Jain style and construction, modified by the addition of domes and arches, is deservedly famous for its delicate and rich ornamentation. The chief monuments are Hilāl Khān Kāzi's mosque at Dholkā (1333 A.D.), the

mosque at Mirzāpur, and the following buildings at
Ahmadābād: the Jām'i Masjid (begun 1426), the
mosque of Mahāfiz Khān (late 15th century), Rāni
Sīparī's mosque and tomb (1514), the Triple Gateway, and the mosque of Sidi Sayyid, renowned for
the delicate tracery of its three stone windows. All
these are in a purely Indian style; but the mosque
and tomb of Nawāb Sardār Khān (1680) is practically Persian. At Sarkhej, six miles from Ahmadābād, is found another important group of mosques
and tombs. The wells, reservoirs, and sluices of
Ahmadābād itself are as beautiful as the mosques.

The most remarkable monument in the Deccan is
the Gol Gumbaz (fig. 162), or tomb of Muhammad
Ādil Shāh (d. 1660). This is a square building with
mīnārs at the corners, and covered with a magnificent dome, the second largest in the world. This
dome is a marvel of engineering skill; its internal
height is 178 feet, and its weight is ingeniously bal-
anced by a system of intersecting pendentives, elegantly avoiding the need for the great masses of
external masonry which appear in most European
buildings of the same type. The tomb is further
remarkable for its boldly projecting cornice, extending 12 feet from the wall at a height of 83 feet from
the ground. The builders of Bījāpur were equally

MUGHAL ARCHITECTURE

dian, at home in his own land. His palace (called the Jahāngīrī Mahall) in the Āgra fort is quite of an Indian type; but the great monument of his time is the city of Fathpur-Sīkrī, built during the fifteen years succeeding 1569, and deserted after its founder's death. The whole city bears the stamp of Akbar's extraordinary genius; as Abūl Fazl well said, "His Majesty plans splendid edifices, and dresses the work of his mind and heart in the garments of stone and clay."

The chief buildings of Fathpur-Sīkrī are the great Mosque, with its immense southern gateway called the Buland Darwāza, or Lofty Gate (fig. 163), and within the enclosed court, more than 300 feet square, the marble tomb of Sheikh Salīm Chishti (fig. 160), with its fairy-like tracery windows, and the marvellous pearl and ebony mosaic of the tomb and canopy within. Scarcely less beautiful are the palaces of the queens, and Akbar's hall of private audience (fig. 165), remarkable for its red sandstone throne, consisting of a great flower-like bracket supported on a single pillar and accessible by galleries above.

Other great works of Akbar's reign are the palace at Allahābād (now greatly injured and more or less inaccessible within the fort), and Akbar's tomb at Sikandra. Concerning this last, a square many-storied building on a raised platform in the centre of a garden, Fergusson makes the interesting suggestion that it was designed on the plan of some then existing Buddhist *vihāra*, and he compares its appearance to that of some of the *rathas* at Māmallapuram. The Panch Mahall at Fathpur-Sīkrī shows a like survival of old Indian design.

Jahāngīr (1605–1628) was not a great builder, like his father and son. His chief work is the palace at Lahore, which in Akbar's reign had already been the capital for fourteen years. To him is also due the tomb of Anārkalī at Lahore, the Shālimār gardens in Kāshmīr, and the eastern capital (in brick) at Dacca. The most beautiful work of this period, however, is the Itīmādu-d-daulah (fig. 164), erected by Nur Jahān, Jahāngīr's wise and beautiful queen, in memory of her father. It is, like the tomb of the Sheikh at Fathpur, wholly in white marble, and covered throughout with inlaid mosaic of coloured stones, the chief decorative motifs being the cypress, Persian water vessels, and flowers. This tomb exhibits a transition from the almost Hindū style of Akbar, to the more Persian style of Shāh Jahān. A Hindū character is still apparent in the roof of the pavilion, which in any more purely Saracenic tomb would have been a dome.

MUGHAL ARCHITECTURE

To the reign of Shāh Jahān belong the Palace at Delhi, the Pearl Mosque at Āgra, and the well-known Tāj Mahall. The last building, one of the most famous and most beautiful in the world, was built by Shāh Jahān during the years 1632–1647, as a tomb and monument for his wife Arjumand Banu Begam, called Mumtāz Mahall (whence by corruption, Tāj Mahall), for twenty years his inseparable companion, and the mother of fourteen of his children, as renowned for her charity as for her beauty. The building, like all living architecture, is due to the co-operation of many craftsmen. There has been much controversy as to the chief or original designer, whether an Italian or a Turk. The matter is of comparatively little importance, as the design is admittedly quite Asiatic, and evidences of Italian influence, even in the decoration, if any, are quite insignificant. It is more noteworthy that the form of the dome is characteristically Indian, the lineal descendant of older Dravidian and Buddhist types, while the ground plan is that of the old Hindū *panch-ratna*—one central dome with four smaller cupolas. Mr Havell utters no paradox when he says that the science of Muhammadan art in India, as well as the inspiration of it, came from the Hindū *Shilpashāstras*.

The Tāj Mahall has not the masculine force of the

Āgra fort; it was meant to be feminine. As Mr E. B. Havell writes : "the whole conception, and every line and detail of it, express the intention of the designers. It is Mumtāz Mahall herself, radiant in her youthful beauty, who still lingers on the banks of the shining Jamna, at early morn, in the glowing mid-day sun, or in the silver moonlight."

The pavilions of white marble, built along the embankment of the lake at Ajmer, are of an exquisite and fairy-like beauty: a fitting place for the entertainment of the lovers who lie together in the Tāj. Nor could anything exceed the delicate purity of the white Pearl Mosque within the Āgra fort, or the magnificence of the buildings which Shāh Jahān added to those of Akbar and Jahāngīr. The palace in the fort at Delhi has been sadly injured in the course of adaptations to the requirements of a modern military barrack.

Architecture, like every other art, declined during the long reign of Aurangzeb; yet many fine buildings, though less important than those already spoken of, were still erected. He was more concerned to do away with Hindū temples, than to raise up buildings of his own. The tall *mīnārs* of the riverside mosque at Benāres, however, are architecturally some compensation for the intolerant vandal-

ism, the spirit of which was one cause of the down-
fall of the Mughal empire in India. After Aurangzeb, the decadence of all considerable architecture
was very rapid; as Mr Vincent Smith truly remarks,
the shoddy buildings of the Nawābs of Oudh are
pretentious abominations. Yet there survived, and
still survives in places such as Mathurā and Delhi,
an eclectic domestic and minor civil style of building of great charm and vitality. It is, however, in
more remote centres—in Rājputāna, Orissa, and the
south, that is to say, outside the main Mughal area,
that fine building traditions have been best preserved: for the Mughal building, however splendid, and
although it made large use of existing technique,
was an artificial growth, dependent on personal patronage, and not, like the Hindū art, a direct
product of local conditions.

CHAPTER ELEVEN
MUGHAL PAINTING & CALLIGRAPHY

172. Jahāngīr. Painting on paper. Size 1⁹⁄₁₂ x 1⁷⁄₁₆ in. 17 c. Mughal.
Museum of Fine Arts, Boston.
173. Hakīm Masih uz-Zāman, by Mīr Hāshim. Brush drawing on
paper. Early 17 c. British Museum.
174. Elephant's head (detail from a *darbar*). Brush drawing on
paper. Abt. 1625. Mughal. Victoria and Albert Museum,
Crown Copyright.
175. Ganj 'Ali Khān and others, surrender of Qandahār (detail).
About 1625. Painted on paper. Mughal. Sītārām Lāl, Benares.

176. Landscape (detail). Mid-17 c. Painting on paper. Mughal. Mahārāja of Benares.

177. Bhīls hunting deer at night. Painting on paper. Mid-17 c. Mughal. Bodleian.

178. Three ladies on a moonlit terrace. Painting on paper. Mid-17 c. Mughal. Bodleian.

179. Carved crystal cups. 2⅛ in., 3¼ in., 2⅛ in. 17 c. Mughal.
    Victoria and Albert Museum, Crown Copyright.
180. *Huka* bowl. *Bidrī*-inlaid gold and silver. 7¼ in. 17 c. Mughal.
    Victoria and Albert Museum, Crown Copyright.
181. *Huka* bowl. Jewelled jade. 7⅜ in. 17 c. Mughal. Victoria and
    Albert Museum, Crown Copyright.
182. Turban ornament (*sarpech*). Jewelled jade. 7¹³⁄₁₆ in. 17 c.
    Mughal. Victoria and Albert Museum, Crown Copyright.
183. Tinned copper ware. (Plate diam. 11½ in.) Copper incised
    and inlaid with black lac. Kāshmīr. Author.
184. Finger-ring. Silver and engraved stone. 17-18 c. Mughal.
    Author.

185. *Huka* bowl. Brass incised and inlaid with black lac. 18-19 c. Panjāb. Victoria and Albert Museum, Crown Copyright.
186. Ewer (*aftāba*). Brass incised and inlaid with black lac. Kāshmīr. Victoria and Albert Museum, Crown Copyright.

187. Box (*Pāndām*). *Bidrī*-inlaid silver. Lucknow (?) 17 c. Victoria and Albert Museum, Crown Copyright.
188. *Huka* bowl. Silver enamel. 18 c. Lucknow. Rai Kishenjī.
189. Enamelled wall tile. 17 c. Earthenware. Lahore. Victoria and Albert Museum, Crown Copyright.

190. Embroidered scarf-end. Wool. 17-18 c. Kāshmīr. Museum of Fine Arts, Boston.
191. Part of woven shawl (twill tapestry). 18-19 c. Kāshmīr. Museum of Fine Arts, Boston.
192. Brocade (*kimkhwāb*). Silk, gold and silver embroidery. Benares. Author.
193. Brocade. Silk, gold and silver embroidery. Benares. Museum of Fine Arts, Boston.
194. Brocade. Silk, gold and silver embroidery. Benares. Museum of Fine Arts, Boston.
195. Part of woven shawl (twill tapestry). Kāshmīr. Early 19 c. Museum of Fine Arts, Boston.

CHAPTER ELEVENTH
MUGHAL PAINTING & CALLIGRAPHY

MUGHAL PAINTING CONSISTS AL-most entirely of book illustrations and portfolio pictures, usually called miniatures. The wall-paintings, of which fragments survive at Fathpur-Sīkrī, are in the same style, and like enlarged miniatures. Mughal painting is a courtly and aristocratic art, realistic and romantic, almost wholly secular, and quite remote from folk-sentiment. It is profoundly interested in individual character, and the splendid ceremonial of court life. Its keynote, accordingly, is portraiture —not the old Asiatic conception of portraiture, the rendering of a type, but actual likeness, verisimilitude. So it happens that we have a remarkable gallery of representations of all the great men of the Mughal times, treated with a quite convincing actuality.

The old home of the Mughals or Tīmūrias was in Turkestān, and it is from the schools of Bukhāra and Samarqand that this interest in personality and character derives. It is by this way also that there enters into Indian Mughal, as into Persian miniature art, a strong Chinese element. The term Indo-Persian is only applicable to a part of the Mughal painting, and obscures its general character. Persia, of course, here means Afghanistān and Turkistān, rather than the south or west. Indo-Tīmūrid would be a better name. But the art, though eclectic, is no mere appendage of the foreign schools; it is quite as distinctive as the Mughal architecture, and, moreover, superior to any Persian art of the 17th century.

The history of Mughal art in India—entirely secular and professional in character—covers little more than a period of two centuries, from the middle of the 16th to the latter part of the 18th century. Its brilliance depended entirely on court and individual patronage. The Tīmūrias had always felt a great interest in art and natural beauty. "It was the season when the garden was in all its glory," writes Bābur, for whom, in the midst of his adventurous life, gardening remained a ruling passion. This interest is reflected in the late 16th-century picture (fig. 166) in which he is represented actually superintending the laying out of a garden.

Next in importance to the Tīmūrid element in Mughal painting is the indigenous Indian; at least three-quarters of the Mughal painters, who often signed their works, bear Hindū names, so that it is not surprising that Rājput elements are often recognisable in Mughal work. Fig. 178, for example, is Rājput in all fundamentals, particularly in physical type, yet there is combined with this a certain romanticism and enhancement of the relief, a con-

228

sciousness of the picturesque, which clearly distinguish it from such purely Rājput work as that of fig. 71. The same romantic interest is apparent in the *Hunting Deer by Night* of fig. 177. There enters also into Mughal art a strong current of direct European influence, sometimes reflected in very ill-advised and unsuccessful attempts at rendering modelling and suggesting relief, more often and more successfully in atmospheric effects and architectural perspective. The beautiful night effects, and the equestrian portraiture, both of which are characteristic of Mughal, but unknown to Persian art, may be developments of suggestions borrowed from European art, or perhaps from indigenous traditions developed under the European influence.

The earliest Indian works are strongly influenced by the school of Bihzād; examples are *Nautch Party of Sultān Muhammad Tughlak*, by Shāpur of Khorāsān (1534 A.D., now at Calcutta), the *Portrait of Sultān Alā-al-dīn* of Bengal (*ca.* 1532 A.D.), British Museum MS., Or. 1372 (fig. 168), and various pictures of the Birth of Jahāngīr, showing the characteristic architecture of Akbar. It was the patronage of Akbar which prepared the way for the development of the characteristic Mughal art of the 17th century. His saying upon painting is well known:

"There are many that hate painting, but such men I dislike. It appears to me as if a painter had quite peculiar means of recognising God; for a painter in sketching anything that has life, and in devising its limbs one after the other, must come to feel that he cannot bestow individuality (a soul) upon his work, and is thus forced to think of God, the Giver of Life, and will thus increase his knowledge."

Akbar employed a large number of Hindū artists to copy the illuminated pictures in the Persian *Shāh Nāmahs* and similar romantic histories; most of these illustrations are in a decadent Persian style of little æsthetic interest. Persian translations of such Indian books as the *Yoga Vāshishtha*, the *Rāmāyana*, and the *Mahābhārata*, however, afforded to the Indian painters a better opportunity for invention, and a new style was thus gradually evolved. In these works the landscape still remains highly artificial, but Indian sentiment predominates in subject-matter and composition. Fig. 171, from a manuscript of the fables of Bidpai (*Kalilah wa Dimnah*, prepared for the last King of Golconda, and dated 1610 A.D.—British Museum, Add. 18579), well illustrates the story-telling quality of these pictures; the buffalo and camel-rider are engaged in conversation regarding the behaviour of men to animals.

MUGHAL PAINTING & CALLIGRAPHY

Of Akbar's time, also, are a number of larger oil-paintings on canvas (fig. 167): there is a good series of these at South Kensington, and one fine example has been lately acquired by the British Museum.

The Mughal portrait style is scarcely clearly developed before the time of Jahāngīr (1605 to 1627). At its best, it is an art of nobly serious realism and deep insight into character; at its worst, it is an art of mere flattery. Two works reproduced here, the Bodleian *Dying Man* (fig. 169) and the Ajmer portrait of *Jadrūp Yogī* (fig. 170), stand out before all others in their passionate concentration. The secular art here attains to a wisdom and insight not less moving than the deep love which inspires Hindū works. It is with the very spirit of the words of the Upanishad—"*Recall, O mind, thy deeds, recall, recall*"—that the dying man is oblivious of everything around and about him, forgetful even of his own emaciated body, while there rise up in his heart pictures of things long past and things to come; while the *Yogī*, seated by the door of his narrow rock-cut cell, naked of all possessions, embodies the thought of that deeper spiritual detachment that seeks to escape from time for ever. In both cases, not merely the character of each individual, but also his intimate relation to an habitual environment, are subtly

231

groups, there are fine examples in all the important collections, *e.g.* the Darbars of Jahāngīr and of Shāh Jahān in the Bodleian MS., Ouseley, Add. 173; the *Farewell of Jahāngīr and Prince Khurram*, by Manohar Singh, India Office, Johnston, Album 4; a *Darbar of Shāh Jahān*, British Museum MS., Add. 18801; a picture by Samand in the collection of the Mahārāja of Benāres (part of which is shown in fig. 176); *Darbar of Jahāngīr*, in the collection of Mr Victor Goloubeff; and the *Surrender of Qandahār* (fig. 175) in the collection of Babu Sītārām Lāl of Benāres. Of single portraits, beside those in various private collections, the best series will be found in the British Museum MS., Add. 18801 (fig. 173). In most of the portraits the head is finished more carefully than any other part; it is rare to meet with suggestions of character in the body or hands. The fineness and realism of the drawing of the features and hair are almost incredible.

In the time of Shāh Jahān there is a tendency to greater suavity and flattery, while the genre pictures and night scenes and equestrian portraits and pictures of ladies become abundant. There are also some good architectural drawings. The landscape is no longer Persian, but shows Indian and European influences (fig. 176). In the reign of Aurangzeb (1658 to 1707) nothing was added to Mughal art, while in the 18th century only a very few works of high merit were produced ; the final decadence in Oudh is not less complete than that of the Mughal architecture. Mughal painting was never deeply rooted in the Indian soil, but rather a purely artificial product of the court and the connoisseurs, a fact which fully accounts for its rapid decline.

It is interesting to note that amongst the 17th-century pictures are quite a large number of Christian subjects, more or less distant copies of Italian originals, as well as imitations of European engravings and secular works of various kinds. On the other hand, we know that Rembrandt was much interested in, and made some copies from, the Indian representations of night scenes. Reynolds seems to have been the first English artist to admire the Mughal paintings. From a later time, there exist copies of Mughal drawings made by Delacroix. Most of the important examples in English collections were brought back after the Mutiny.

Amongst the 17th- and 18th-century pictures there are also many of Hindū subjects, usually night scenes. The Mughal interest in the picturesque, and the general tolerance up to the time of Aurangzeb, no doubt enabled them to take as much interest in the Hindū as in the Christian subjects, while the former must also have appealed to the many Hindūs present at the Mughal court, and to those in Rājputāna as far as Mughal court fashions penetrated.

While the Persians after the 13th century, and the Mughals in India, were not troubled overmuch by orthodox scruples forbidding the representation of living things, it resulted from the old Islāmic Puritanism that their art became entirely secular. Religious motifs from Islām are scarcely ever treated in Mughal art : though there are some beautiful pictures dealing with the subject-matter of the mystical romances, the favourite story being that of the separated lovers Lailā and Majnūn.

Part of an inscription at Gaur (Fath Khān's Mosque near Maldah, 1524 A.D.). After Ravenshaw.

The art of calligraphy, or fair-writing, so long cultivated by the Persians, was not less highly esteemed at the Mughal court. The emperors possessed important libraries of earlier MSS. brought from Turkestan, which they constantly enlarged by the addition of contemporary work. The earlier Indo-Persian

MSS. are sometimes of great magnificence, though scarcely equal to those of Bokhāra and Samarqand in splendour and perfection of design. It is rather in the making of illuminated texts that the Mughal calligraphers excelled ; these brilliant pages are found with the portfolio pictures and albums, and were valued almost as highly, perhaps more highly, than the actual pictures.

In this connection, it is important to note that Persian painting from its beginning in the 13th century has always been more or less calligraphic; painting and writing went hand in hand, with strong reciprocal influences. These conditions obtained also with the Mughals in India; they represent a well-marked distinction of Mughal painting, alike from the older art of fresco, and from the true Rājput art, its later descendant. Painting and writing amongst the Hindūs were quite independent arts. It is scarcely ever that one meets with an illustrated Sanskrit or vernacular Hindū MS. ; while the distinction between the monumental severity of the *Deva-Nāgarī*, and the flowing grace of the Persian script is very obvious.

In conclusion, it will be worth while to note the names of a few of the more important of the Mughal painters of the late 16th and earlier 17th centuries.

MUGHAL PAINTING & CALLIGRAPHY

School of Akbar :—Bhagvatī, Daswant, Nanhā, Basāwan, Abdul Samad, Farrukh, Tirriyya, Sarwan, Miskīn, Jagannāth.

School of Jahāngīr and Shāh Jahān :—Hunhār, Samand, Anūpchitar, Chitarman, Manohar Singh, Mansūr, Muhammad Afzal, Muhammad Nādir of Samarqand, Mīr Hāshim, Fakirullah Khān, Dhan Sah.

CHAPTER TWELVE
OF THE MINOR MUGHAL ARTS

CHAPTER TWELFTH
OF THE MINOR MUGHAL ARTS

TO DISTINGUISH ABSOLUTELY BETween Mughal and Hindū arts is naturally not always possible. Just as in architecture, so for example in weaving, design and tradition overlap and interpenetrate. We shall only describe here, therefore, such arts as are most typically Mughal in design and application, without implying that any or all of them were unknown to India at an earlier period.

Amongst the most characteristic of the Mughal crafts are those connected with the hard and semiprecious stones. Perhaps most exquisite of all are the cups and bowls of carved crystal, of which fine examples are illustrated in fig. 179. These cups, with those of green and white jade, some Persian glass and enamels, and some blue china, formed the table service of the Mughal aristocracy. The art of inlaying jade with precious stones, held fast by a gold bezel, was applied to *huka* bowls, sword handles, and jewellery. Such personal possessions as archers' thumb-rings, *huka* mouthpieces, and rosaries are often made of jade, carved or inlaid. Still better known is the application of stone-inlay on a larger scale to the decoration of buildings of the 17th century, especially the Tāj Mahall; it is applied also to marble pavements such as that of the baths in the palace at

Delhi, and to minor objects such as carpet-weights. Seal engraving (also an old Hindū art) was extensively practised under the Mughals; jewels, particularly emerald, but also ruby, were delicately carved and engraved.

Enamelling in the Mughal period had its centres at Jaipur, Delhi, and afterwards at Lucknow. The distinction between Rājput and Mughal enamelled jewellery is slight, as there was much Mughal influence at Jaipur. The Lucknow enamelling is mostly

Side of a Lucknow silver-enamel box.

of the 18th century, and easily distinguished from that of Jaipur by its different range of colour, green, brown, and blue on a silver ground, in place of the deep red, green, and ivory-white of Jaipur, with but little metal visible. The *huka* bowl of fig. 188 is a fine example of Lucknow enamel, with well-drawn trees and birds and animals. There are also elegant silver boxes decorated with peacocks or doves; sword furniture, *pāndāns*, and jewellery. Silver and niello boxes of excellent design were also made at Lucknow in the 18th century. There are some painted enamels in a Persian style. Some fair enamel in blue and white is made at Multān.

Amongst the most important types of metal-work are the various kinds of *bidrī* damascening, applied to pitchers, basins, betel-boxes (*pāndāns*) (fig. 187), and *huka* bowls. *Bidrī* is an old Hindū art, so called from Bidar, in the Deccan; it was extensively patronised by the Mughals, so that it is now best known as a Musulmān art, practised in Lucknow, though *bidrī* continued to be made by Hindūs in Bengal (Purniah) and in Bidar.

Almost equally handsome are some of the brass *huka* bowls and pitchers (figs. 185, 186). It may be noted here that the round bowls (figs. 180, 181) belong to the 17th century, those with a broad flat base (fig. 188) to the 18th. Some of the best Mughal metal work is found in the tinned copper ware of Kāshmīr (fig. 183); here the designs are engraved, and filled in with a black composition before the vessel is tinned; so that the design finally stands out in black on a silver ground. Many of the Kāshmīr vessels are of admirable form and design, and handsomely engraved with inscriptions.

The architectural use of coloured tiles was known in early times (Anurādhapura, Peshāwar, etc.); but its extensive use under the Mughals is certainly a result of external influences. The palace of Mān Singh at Gwaliar, however, was once profusely decorated with glazed tiles of purely Hindū design. Most of the true Mughal tiling is of the kind called *kāshī* or *chīnī*, made of separate pieces laid as a mosaic. The Chīnī-ka-Rauzah, a poet's tomb at Āgra, though much damaged, retains enough of its enamelled covering to show what splendour this form of decoration attained. In the same technique is the brilliant tiled wall in the Lahore fort 500 yards in length and 16 high, "the most remarkable series of tile pictures in the world." These, with the mosque of Wazīr Khān and other works at Lahore decorated in the same manner, all belong to the second quarter of the 17th century. This mosaic tile-work was preceded in the 16th and early 17th centuries by the beautiful square tiles of Lahore made of earthenware painted in enamel with designs of animals and flowers (fig. 189). After the 17th century, again, the mosaic style was replaced by an inferior imitation of the enamelled work. The tile-work of the Sind, and especially Multān, is characterised by its extensive use of white and blue; the industry goes back to the 13th century, but little is now done except the decoration of ornamental vases.

The ivory carving of Delhi is quite a modern

industry, and, like the painting on ivory panels, more of a trade than an art : and there is little ivory work of much importance surviving from the Mughal period. The best examples are *qalamdāns* or pen-boxes carved with floral designs in shallow panels.

An art which attained very great perfection under the Mughals was that of mother-of-pearl and ebony mosaic, one of the many sorts of inlay and marquetry that have been practised in different times or places in India. The most perfect example is that of the canopy over the tomb of Sheikh Salīm Chishti (1581 A.D.), at Fathpur-Sīkrī. The work is of extraordinary intricacy; each tiny piece of shell or ebony is cut to the required shape, and fastened with minute pins and shellac; the edges of the mouldings are bound with copper. Something of the same kind of work is seen in the well-known inlaid boxes of Bombay, in which, however, the design is monotonous and too minute; the technique here is of Persian origin.

Much is heard of Indian carpets; but it may be doubted whether the art of making woollen-pile carpets can be considered as in any sense indigenous. It is certain that beautiful carpets were made in Mughal times at Lahore and in Jaipur, and very likely also at Delhi and Āgra, as well as in Masulipatam and Haiderābād. The latter half of the 19th century marked the complete decadence of Indian carpet-weaving, due to two causes—the Western trade demand for cheapness, and the manufacture of inferior sorts in gaols. Of late years there has been a revival of good work at Amritsar and Āgra and in several gaols. Woollen-pile carpets would be uncomfortably warm at all seasons in Central and Southern India; a far more agreeable floor-covering is afforded by the smooth cotton *darīs* without pile.

Cotton-printing is an art common to the Persian and Hindū cultures. The Persian influence is clear in the work of Lahore, Lucknow, and many other places in the north, though in most parts of Rājputāna there survive distinctively Hindū traditions. Amongst the finest works in which there is a combination of block-printing and dye-painting are the *palampores* of Masulipatam, where a small manufacture still survives, with an export trade to Persia. It would be difficult to exaggerate the beauty of the Masulipatam designs, or to praise too highly their rich glowing colour; some of the best are still made, uncontaminated by chemical dyes. The Persian influence is here strong; but there are other types of southern cotton-printing in which Hindū motifs alone appear; this applies to most of the printed *sārīs* or dress-pieces, as well as to the temple ceiling cloths. Close relations exist between the designs of the painted or printed cottons, and those of painted ceilings.

The first knowledge of silk is Chinese, and though it has been known in India since the early days of Chinese trade with the West, certainly since the 4th century B.C., the greater part of the splendid silken fabrics of Northern India are strongly influenced by Persian design. Thus, the famous *kimkhwāb* silk-brocade weavers of Benāres are Musulmāns, and trace their origin to immigration in the time of Mahmūd of Ghaznī, in the 10th century; according to their own story, they introduced the use of gold thread, and before that time the Hindūs wove only plain cloth. In any case, the use of gold thread —thin flat gold strips of pure gold or silver gilt twisted round a silk core, as distinct from solid gold wire—does not date further back than the 11th century. The usual types of design are those peculiarly beautiful repeating patterns of addorsed or affronted creatures, with the tree of life, the diapers, and floral sprays, which we are familiar with in the Sicilian and Old Italian brocades, all based on Oriental patterns which preserve Old Assyrian designs (figs. 192–4). The colour and texture of the Indian

247

silks, whether of Benāres, Surāt, Ahmādabād, or Lahore, are of quite extraordinary richness, and not less permanent than brilliant. But it is scarcely possible to find a single piece of modern silk, either of pure rich colour, or of fine quality, at once soft and heavy.

Designs of Benāres *kimkhwābs*.

All work in leather is in the hands of Musulmāns or the lowest castes of Hindūs, since it is for Hindūs an unclean material. Orthodox Brāhmans, for instance, prefer wooden to leather sandals; but the latter are made in all parts of India. A good plain type is that of Kāshmīr, where leather socks and strapwork sandals are largely worn. Embroidered and dyed shoes of excellent design are still made in Delhi, Lucknow, and Amritsar. Fine leather

248

water-vessels are made in Bīkaner, and decorated with gesso, coloured; leather bottles for oil are used by Hindūs. A familiar sight in India is the Musulmān water-carrier, who waters streets and gardens from a vessel made from a whole skin of a sheep. Many parts of Rājputāna, the Panjāb, and Kāshmīr, produce fine embroidered saddlery and trappings. The embroidered deer-skin sheets of Haiderābād Sind, and the Udaipur belts are even more characteristic. It may be noted that an exception to the Hindū avoidance of leather is seen in the case of *yogīs*, whose traditional seat or rug is a deer-skin; and Shiva himself, as the Great Yogī, is often represented as clothed in the skins of animals.

The best known Musulmān embroideries are those of Delhi, Āgra, and Benāres in gold and silver wire and silk. These are often executed on heavy materials such as velvets, or satins lined with cotton, and used for coats, collars, and other sumptuary purposes. Such work is often overloaded, especially when gold spangles are freely used. Far more refined are the white quilted coats of Baluchistān and Chitral, the *soznis* of Peshāwar (and Bokhāra), and the less known but fine domestic *kasīda* embroidery in *tasar* silk on cotton, of Bengal and Western India; the latter craft, like many other Musulmān domestic textile crafts of

embroidery and plaiting in the West, shows clear
Arabian influences. Good white embroidery of the
chikan type is sometimes seen on the *burqas* or huge
enveloping veils worn by orthodox Musulmān ladies
(Bhopal, etc.) when they go abroad.

But of all Indian textiles, none excel in beauty of
colour, texture, and design, the famous Kāshmīr
shawls. Space will allow no more than a mention
of the plain blankets, serges, and felts of Bīkaner and
Kāngrā, Amritsar, and other places in the Panjāb.
All the finest work has come from Kāshmīr, and
takes the forms of shawls and coats (*chogas*); some
of these are woven, some embroidered, the result
being often indistinguishable without close inspec-
tion or an examination of the reverse side of the
stuff. The woven shawls are all of patchwork construction, though the joins are so fine as to be in-
visible, and the thickness of the stuff is not affected
at the join. Such shawls are made of long strips or
ribbons woven as fine tapestry on small looms, and
afterwards joined along their length: but many of
the best shawls are partly woven and partly embroidered. The finest work appears more like painting
than tapestry; and the most costly may be worth as
much as or more than a thousand pounds. The usual
motif of the decoration of the woven shawls is the

well-known cone or "shawl pattern" (figs. 191, 195), derived, almost certainly, from the Persian wind-blown cypress. An embroidered scarf, illustrating the story "Shirīn-Farhād," is illustrated in fig. 190. Since the Kāshmīr famine of 1833 a large part of the industry has been located in the Panjāb. No work of any importance is done now; in fact, no part of India produces more banal and meaningless embroidery than present-day Kāshmīr, where the tradesman's chief pride is taken in realistic green *chenar* leaves executed in floss silk on cotton for sale to tourists.

A Kāshmīr craft which is less degenerate, though very little fine work is still made, is that of painted papier-maché. Sheets of paper are pasted on to moulds of the required form, and painted and varnished; the older examples were so well made as to hold even hot liquids. Most of the present-day work is really painted wood.

The fashions of Muhammadan costume in India before the Mughals were more or less purely Persian. The Mughals, however, at least from Akbar to Shāh Jahān, were thoroughly Indian in their tastes; and their costume, both of men and women, was taken over almost completely from the Rājputs, as the pictures clearly testify. Thus the Mughal turbans differ from the contemporary Bokhāra types in not having the loose fringed ends sticking out on both sides; they are smaller and neater. The Indian coat fastening at the side, as in China, is quite different from the long Persian gown that buttons all down the centre and fits closely to the form; the Indian coats also develop large and full skirts. The skirt, bodice, and veil of Rājput ladies prevailed in the Mughal zenanas of the 17th century, but with constant change of fashion in respect of details.

INDEX